I0104607

The Ramblings of an Incoherent Fool

By: Neth Rushlo

Copyright © 2011 by Kenneth L. Rushlo, Jr. and www.Lulu.com

All rights reserved. This book or any portion thereof may not be reproduced or used in any manner whatsoever without the express written permission of the publisher except for the use of brief quotations in a book review.

Printed in the United States of America

First Printing, 2011

ISBN 978-1-257-83395-5

www.Lulu.com

This is dedicated to my first love Scott. Thank you for coming into my life and allowing me to experience your love. I could not have asked for anyone better. You shall always remain in my heart and mind forever.

Table of Contents

Prelude

Jean-Claude had not been feeling well lately and had been keeping himself busy with work and volunteering with different drag shows in different parts of Southern California. Jean-Claude had befriended a drag queen by the stage name of Ms. Wauneta several years ago and was visiting with her at her house. Jean-Claude knocked on the door and quickly heard a deep voice rumble, "Come in Chickie." Jean-Claude instantaneously knew Bill had not started his transformation into Ms. Wauneta because he was using his male voice. As Jean-Claude entered the apartment, Bill was padding out of the kitchen in his pink frilly housecoat with pink slippers carrying a cup of hot coffee. Handing the cup to Jean-Claude Bill said, "As you see Ms. Wauneta is a little late appearing this morning. Let's head to the mirror to see how much spackle this old face needs to cover up all the wrinkles." Jean-Claude laughed and followed down the hall to the "production room" as Bill called it.

Bill sat down at the makeup table and looked in the mirror at Jean-Claude. "Okay, what is wrong with you Chickie? Why don't you come over here and tell Ms. Wauneta about it, we have time since I think she is going to be stubborn today and getting her out of bed is not going to be an easy task." while patting an ottoman sitting near the makeup table. Jean-Claude sat down and sighed, "I don't think we have that much time Bill." Bill looked at Jean-Claude in the mirror again and softly said, "I always have time to listen to you honey. You just start talking and Ms. Wauneta will interject when she needs to, trust me." With that Jean-Claude began talking:

The Awakening

Germany

Jean-Claude, just 17-years old, blond hair, blue eyes, slender and firm body from months of training in basic and AIT. Jean-Claude might have weighed 125 pounds, soaking wet. He was from a small village in Michigan consisting, at most, 1,300 people. Jean-Claude thought, "Finally off that plane and now to find food, a hot shower and a place to sleep, don't care what order it comes either." Jean-Claude enlisted in the Army at 16, obtaining a waiver because of being underage. Away from his family and drill instructions, Jean-Claude could now begin his life.

After hauling the heavy duffle bag from one end of the airport to the front, Jean-Claude was exhausted. He finally sat down, waiting for the van to pick him up and take him to 3d Infantry Division. Division Headquarters was located in Wurzburg where he would receive his assignment to his new company. Jean-Claude began thinking of the long flight; "How many hours was that flight...we left at...ah who cares?" Finally, a green van was making its way around the corner. "Wait a minute, that is a VW panel van," Jean-Claude thought with amusement, "only in Germany." The van pulled up and a Private First Class asked his name and looked at his papers and said, "Get in and we'll go to Division." That be the Army, just the facts and let's go. Jean-Claude thought the PFC looked irritated as having had drawn the short end of the detail stick to come and pick him up at the airport in the middle of the night. You see, the Army likes moving personnel around in the middle of night, maybe that is when the cheap flights are available, and it's not for any convenience of personnel.

As the van was pulling up to Division Headquarters all Jean-Claude could think was, "finally, where do I sleep," he wasn't hungry any longer since it was 0300 in the morning. The PFC told him to go into the Staff Duty Officers office and wait for quarters. Finally, after initial check-in an AO (Area of Occupation) was assigned at 0530. The long day was just starting, breakfast was already being served in the mess hall and formal check-in was at 0800. Jean-Claude went to the mess hall and ate; wolfing down the food as he was still in the "basic training" thinking of eating fast and get out. After eating Jean-Claude had a few hours to kill before check-in; so he went to the AO to get a little sleep. Sleep came fast and hard, the next he knew was the alarm on his watch was going off to get up.

After arriving at check-in Jean-Claude was to wait seven days before transfer to his permanent duty station. Relieved Jean-Claude could relax and sleep for a week before going to a new duty station. Jean-Claude never left the Kaserne for the entire week; even though he knew an entire new world was out there just waiting to for exploration.

After a relaxing week of doing nothing but watching TV, eating and sleeping it was time to pack up and head to the new duty station. Jean-Claude found out he was going to be attached to a mechanized infantry unit; "Shit, what a crappy assignment," Jean-Claude thought. Being assigned to a mechanized infantry unit was not on the top of Jean-Claude's dream assignments.

When military personnel are in route; they seldom know where they are going or when they will arrive at the final destination. This move was no different from others; however, the military is efficient at moving personnel around with little notice. This time a different PFC had been charged with driving Jean-Claude the two hours from Division located in Wurzburg to Aschaffenburg. Jean-Claude's new duty station was to be 1/7 Infantry Battalion nestled inside the town of Aschaffenburg. Jean-Claude would spend the next three years here. The

Kasernes scattered throughout Aschaffenburg. There was Graves Kaserne, where 1/7 was located with the 26th Support Group, Ready Kaserne, Jaeger Kaserne and a couple others Jean-Claude didn't know. Jaeger Kaserne housed Brigade Headquarters where Jean-Claude was dumped off by the PFC with a smart, "Go in that door, up the stairs to the left and check in."

Standing in front of Brigade Headquarters, Jean-Claude looked around at the buildings; it was as if he was standing in postcard someone might have sent when they visited Germany. Clean, long white buildings three stories tall with reddish clay tile roofs. Finally, up the stairs he went, looking for the Duty Officer to check him in and get transport to his new unit. After a few hours a Specialist showed up in the door and said, "Let's go." Jean-Claude missed the Specialist's name. Additionally, Jean-Claude never saw him again. This was sometimes the nature of the military most of the time, one can have interactions with countless people that they will never see nor get to know at all even on the same base.

Next stop was Battalion Headquarters on Graves Kaserne roughly one mile from Jaeger Kaserne. Again, Jean-Claude trudged up more stairs to a Staff Duty office. There, his assignment was to be with A Company, 1/7 Infantry. The Staff NCO pointed to a building and said, "Go see the CQ (Charge of Quarters) up on the first floor of A Company." (CQ is a duty that few liked since the desk was staffed by a rotating list of NCOs and enlisted on a 24-hour shift.) Jean-Claude arrived at Alpha Company and advised the duty NCO of his assignment in Alpha and gave a copy of his orders. The runner was dispatched to get the First Sergeant and while waiting the normal amount of razzing began whenever entering a new duty station. People would pass with normal comments of "Who is the new meat?" "Ah, look another friggin' cherry." Jean-Claude didn't comment, knowing this was just simple banter all the while thinking, "They have no idea who or what I am." Jean-Claude took comfort in that thought since he knew once they figured out he was their new Supply Clerk they would change their attitudes.

The barracks were old WWII German barracks the United States took from the Germans at the end of WWII. The buildings were long and the hallways had grooved cement centers. If you walked on them in socks or bare feet your feet would hurt when you arrived at the latrines found at either end of the building. Showers located in the middle of each floor with boilers for hot water located in the basement with platoon leaders' offices. Alpha Company's building was unique as it also housed the JAG offices on the first floor; so Alpha only had the basement, second and third floors for quarters. Men were stuffed into available rooms. The fourth floor contained the alert lockers for those members staying off base, a storage room for supply to keep bedding and a recreation room for the Company. The second floor was split between offices for the Commander, XO, First Sergeant, supply, Headquarters Platoon and part of First Platoon. Alpha Company was the only Company in Battalion short one floor. Behind the CQ desk was a photo of the Alpha Company building taken during WWII with a German company standing in front of the building. If a person peered closely, they would be able to make out the Swastika above the front door.

Finally the First Sergeant arrived and called Jean-Claude into the office. Jean-Claude was asked a few cursory questions and with a quick glance at the orders the First Sergeant said, "Ah, I see you are the new Supply Clerk. Well welcome and let's get you settled into your AO and then you can meet your new boss." Yelling out the door to the CQ the First Sergeant began barking orders, "CQ, get the keys to room 112 and send the runner to get Sergeant Bird posthaste." Jean-Claude was given keys and taken to his new AO.

Jean-Claude was thinking as he entered the room, "Whew, I'm finally at the last stop, just need to unpack, make the bed and settle in a bit before this Sergeant Bird appeared." The room was of satisfactory size. It contained two bunk beds, four wall lockers, a couch facing the two windows and a television between the windows. Under each window was an old fashioned radiator; on top of each was a canteen cup with water to keep the humidity in the room up during operation. Since it was the middle of the day, it was fairly quiet in the barracks. After about 30 minutes there was a knock at the door and Sergeant Bird poked his head in the door, "Are you Jean-Claude?" Jean-Claude looked at this medium build older man and said, "Yes, Sergeant." Sergeant Bird was looking at Jean-Claude with keen interest and said, "Okay, well let's go and get you up and running we need to carry out a few things today." Jean-Claude hurried to stuff his gear into the locker, throw a lock on the door and hurry after the Sergeant. As Jean-Claude was closing the room door, he glanced down the hall at Sergeant Bird halfway down the long corridor all Jean-Claude could think, "Damn he is fast." Jean-Claude ran down the hall after the sergeant.

Jean-Claude rounded the corner and entered a room at the end of the hall looking much like his AO. The difference was this room had two desks and six huge lockers with a shelving unit by the door stretching along the wall full of wool blankets, sheets and pillow cases. These items were used for resupplying the unit on laundry day. Sergeant Bird quickly looked at Jean-Claude and in a matter of fact tone said, "This is our home." This was the beginning of nine months working with Sergeant Bird.

Sergeant Bird was an interesting fellow, standing about 5'7", roughly 180 pounds and stocky he reminded Jean-Claude of a fireplug. Drafted during Vietnam, Sergeant Bird chose to stay committed to the military until retirement. The relationship that developed between Sergeant Bird and Jean-Claude was, in Jean-Claude's mind, one of father and son. Jean-Claude would have gone to the ends of the earth for this man. Jean-Claude quickly settled into the day-to-day routines required, learning quickly everything needed to keep a company running smoothly. The schedule in garrison was easy enough: wake at 0430, first formation at 0500, Physical Training (PT) at 0510, returning around 0600. After showers head to the mess hall for breakfast, then house chores and finally work formation at 0800 then off to work for the day.

During this period Jean-Claude was getting settled when things began to happen. This cause Jean-Claude to become confused and disoriented between his head and his feelings. Jean-Claude began compartmentalizing things to keep them separate and manageable. This period would also begin the awakening of a young gay man.

Brad

It was while pulling duty at the mess hall, about three weeks after arrival in Alpha Company, taking down meal authorization card numbers that Jean-Claude met Brad. One day towards the end of meal service Brad was the last person to check into the mess hall as Jean-Claude was packing up to eat himself. Brad said, "Why don't you join me for dinner." Jean-Claude, not giving it much thought replied, "Sure." The conversation that began at dinner around 1800 ended around 0130 that night. The two spoke of growing up, likes, and dislikes, news items, politics (which was always a hot topic between these two) and duty assignments. Jean-Claude liked Brad, who was a nice guy that Jean-Claude found they had a lot in common.

> Ms. Wauneta interjected, "Ah there we go, spackle all finished; now for the artwork portion of our program." Turning and looking at Jean-Claude she said, "Finally we are getting somewhere with this story. This better get juicy honey, Ms. Wauneta likes guys named Brad; they are cute little buggers." Jean-Claude laughed since Ms. Wauneta had been with a great guy named Brad for almost 25 years before he passed away.

Brad was 5'9", between 160 and 170 pounds, in great shape, intelligent and was a load of fun to be around. Jean-Claude hung out with Brad every chance he got and they began a very tight bond that only comes from being in the military – Brad was the brother Jean-Claude never really had. Jean-Claude and Brad would go out to the clubs on Fridays or stay and hang out in the bowling alley drinking and just having a good time together. Brad had a girlfriend back in the states and they were always continuously fighting through the US Mail. See this was all before Internet, Email, and cell phones arrived which we take for granted now. Whenever Jean-Claude saw Brad with a letter from his woman, he knew there would be drinking going on either that night or the next available free time to drink.

Brad was assigned to Delta Company, as the Company Clerk. This allowed Jean-Claude and he to keep same schedules and seldom pulled duty outside the normal work. There are perks to getting plum assignments like Company Clerk, or being a driver for officers, almost any position in Headquarters Platoon in a company held the assignments everyone wanted. It would mean no duty assignments late at night or weekends, extra time off, better living quarters and shielded from the normal life of infantry. Brad had a sadistic First Sergeant that he was always complaining to Jean-Claude about and Jean-Claude simply listened because he knew Brad was just blowing off steam. All the while, Jean-Claude just stared at Brad and was thinking how beautiful his eyes and smile were, until Jean-Claude would come to his senses and block out those thoughts.

May Day was fast arriving, and anyone who has lived in Germany knows what a big deal this holiday is to the German people. Brad had family friends that lived in a town about an hour's drive away and asked Jean-Claude if he wanted to go and visit. Jean-Claude readily agreed and suggested that he ask Sergeant Bird if he could borrow his car and would let Brad know. See Jean-Claude had a European Driver's License, a valuable card when in the military and difficult for military personnel to hold. Every member of the military operating any vehicle was required to have a European Driver's License. Sergeant Bird readily agreed to let Jean-Claude borrow the car for the weekend.

Come Friday night, both Brad and Jean-Claude packed the car and headed off into the night on an adventure. Jean-Claude asked Brad how he knew these people, since it could have been in any number of ways because American soldiers were always making German friends. Brad told Jean-Claude about his father having been shot down flying over Germany in WWII. This family found him and hid his father for several months before being able to smuggle him back across battle lines to the Americans. The family was taking a huge risk with their own lives to succeed with this humanitarian deed of hiding and helping an American soldier. This struck Jean-Claude hard and would forever be in his mind the rest of his life.

Jean-Claude and Brad finally arrived at the family friends and they already had dinner waiting for them when they came through the door. As you can imagine a typical family, but this being a special occasion, both May Day and Brad attending as well. They accepted Jean-Claude into their family as if they had known him all their life. Jean-Claude could not have been happier and enjoyed the evening speaking both German and English about several topics with three different generations of this new family.

As the night wore down the family put Brad and Jean-Claude to bed upstairs in their own room which had two separate beds. Jean-Claude thought, "Phew, at least I don't have to worry about the sleeping arrangement."

> Ms. Wauneta waived a big powder brush at Jean-Claude with an evil grin and said, "Oh come now, would it have been so bad to sleep next to a hot military man?"

The next morning the family woke the two up with the smells of coffee, pancakes, bacon and laughter. Jean-Claude woke in the morning thinking, "It is nice to be home" before remembering he was in Germany. As Brad was getting out of bed, Jean-Claude glanced over and saw Brad standing in just his bikini underwear for the first time. Jean-Claude immediately thought, "Oh God, what a beautiful man." Black hair, brown eyes, olive skin, firm toned body, medium built chest to sculpted abs, bubble butt, and a large bulging package as well. This drove Jean-Claude's entire mind into overdrive as Brad was groggily stumbling towards the bathroom to take a shower. The image seared itself into Jean-Claude's mind to such an extent that he will never forget that scene. Jean-Claude became aroused and kept running the short film of Brad walking across the room naked over and over in his head.

> "Oh my, I feel the vapors coming on now." As Ms. Wauneta started waiving a handheld fan on her face. "Honey, Ms. Wauneta could just eat this man up you know, in my younger days…oh hell, who am I kidding I'd eat him up now." Jean-Claude just laughed and continued.

Finally, Brad came out of the bathroom with just a white towel around his waist. Instantly, Jean-Claude turned, looked and just about fell over, Brad was a God in Jean-Claude's eyes. Again, the beautifully sculpted body was on display and Brad had no idea what was happening in Jean-Claude's mind. Jean-Claude quickly darted off to the bathroom before his thoughts were revealed by a growing member down south. Jean-Claude took a shower thinking of the image of Brad. "What the hell is happening to me," Jean-Claude thought, "Why do I find Brad so damn hot and sexy?" "You are not supposed to like guys dude!" "What is wrong with you?" "Okay, you need to get this under control before you go out that door or you are going to be in of trouble." "If Brad ever found out this is what you are thinking about him, he will never speak with you again." Jean-Claude's mind was entering the meltdown stages of thinking. So many thoughts were rushing in and no way to sort them out with no time to deal with anything. Jean-Claude simply opened a box and stuffed his thoughts and feelings inside; shut the lid and got out of the bathroom.

When Jean-Claude left the bathroom, Brad was sitting on the edge of Jean-Claude's bed, and looked at Jean-Claude with an irksome glare saying, "What took so long, playing with yourself?" Jean-Claude turned beet red and just rushed to the other side of the bed to throw on his clothes. Jean-Claude couldn't look at Brad; tears were welling up in his eyes as he hurriedly threw on his clothes. Jean-Claude felt awful for thinking of his best friend sexually and felt as if he had let Brad down. Finally, Jean-Claude was ready and said, "Okay, let's go ass."

Going down the stairs to breakfast, Jean-Claude got a good look at Brad's ass as he descended the stairs and the thoughts he had in the bathroom all came rushing back. Jean-Claude just kept thinking, "Get the lid on that box and get this under control." When they entered the dining room, everything stuffed into his mental box and everything was normal. Jean-Claude relieved to have the distractions of breakfast and everyone making plans for the day to distract him from his thoughts.

"Oh Chickie, your first man-crush, how cute." Ms. Wauneta said. Jean-Claude glared and snapped, "Will you just be quiet, and you are not helping here." "Okay, okay. Testy we are this morning." while going back to applying more makeup to her face.

An hour had passed and the daughter of the family said, "Okay, it is time to go, you will find a bike on the side of the house." Jean-Claude looked at Brad with surprise and said "You never mentioned bikes, what is all this about?" The daughter replied, "We always go bike riding on May Day, you will have fun, don't worry." Jean-Claude frustrated and not amused tried to hide his face by looking down at the floor and following Brad out the door. Lying against the side of the house were twelve bikes. They all began the chore of untangling and picking out which bike to whom they would go. It became even funnier when Mother got involved in assigning bikes. In her broken English she was clearly in charge of this assignment and took it very serious. Obviously there was a schedule that one must adhere to this day. Brad and Jean-Claude just looked at one another and began laughing at the sight of each other on these bikes. They had been given tall bikes and could barely sit on the bike while touch the ground even on tippy-toe. "This was going to be an interesting day," Jean-Claude thought. Little did he know how true this statement was until much later in the day.

As they were leaving the house Brad asked about the other bikes left at the house and Mother replied, "Those are for the people who are late, they will have to catch up." Another lesson in German punctuality at its best! When they left the house it was promptly 1000 and had barely ridden three miles when Jean-Claude noticed the first riders were pulling over, "hmm, what is this?" he thought. As Jean-Claude approached he slowed the bike down somehow managing to launch himself off the bike a just before it stopped tilting it enough so he didn't get racked in the nuts. Brad almost fell over laughing at the site of Jean-Claude trying to get off the bike. As Jean-Claude looked up, he realized they had stopped at a bar, he looked at Brad and Brad just shrugged his shoulders as if he was saying, "Just roll with it." Jean-Claude and Brad had developed this unique ability to, for the most part; know what each other was thinking without saying a word.

Entering the bar Brad and Jean-Claude met the first group of the caravan already sitting down. As they approached one member of the group said, "Sit down, drinks are on the way." Jean-Claude began thinking, "Not even 1030 and a drink; oh well here goes nothing." When the drinks arrived they were a full German pilsner glass of heavy beer. (Anyone who has been to Germany knows just how big and potent these beers can be, especially the heavy dark beers.) While they were drinking, the four late members of the group entered laughing and saying, "See I told you they were in here. Mother, you could have waited a couple of minutes we were not that far behind." Mother replied, "You know the way and we don't want to be late, speaking of which we need to get moving." So everyone drank up and headed off down the road.

The group had gotten about five more miles down the road and again the caravan was pulling off the road. Jean-Claude yelled to Brad, "What is it this time?" Brad looked back and said, "Not sure." It was another bar, the ritual was repeated; bikes stacked, enter, drinks were on the way, sit, drink, talk, and back to the bikes. This went on for the next six hours; Brad and Jean-Claude were both getting drunk quickly. Soon they both lost count of the number of bars and drinks they had. All they knew towards the end of the day was that they were at least heading in the right direction to get back to the house.

Roughly one mile from the house Brad was looking back at Jean-Claude and said, "Would you hurry it up." When he suddenly began heading towards the ditch, Jean-Claude shouted, "Look where you are going before you end in the drink." It was too late, between Brad's speed, the alcohol and just being Brad, in the ditch he went flying through the air and landing in the water at the bottom of the ditch. Jean-Claude rode up, got off the bike laughing and looking down at a soaking wet Brad who was laughing as well. Jean-Claude went down to help Brad out of the water and Brad grinned and quickly pulled him into the water with him. Completely soaked both Brad and Jean-Claude began wrestling around in the mud and water all the while laughing hysterically. Jean-Claude looked at Brad and he felt his heart slam against his chest as they just looked at each other laughing and smiling. Jean-Claude wanted to just kiss Brad on the mouth as he looked down at Brad's chest with his shirt sticking to his chest and Jean-Claude pushed away from Brad. All Jean-Claude could think about was to run, get as far away from Brad as possible.

Finally, both arrived at the house and everyone was laughing at the site of two grown men soaked to the bone with mud all over them, grass in their hair, and just looking silly. Mother quickly turned the garden hose on to spray them down before they were allowed to step foot into the house. After getting cleaned up, food was had and it was off to bed for the night. Both guys slept off their drunken stupor only to wake in the morning with a screaming headache.

Finally it came time to go back to Aschaffenburg and goodbyes said and off they went. Brad and Jean-Claude talked about how much fun they had this weekend the entire trip back home. Arriving back home was sad for Jean-Claude because he didn't want to be away from Brad. As Jean-Claude quietly entered his room, so not to wake up his roommates, he kept thinking of Brad. All those thoughts he stuffed in the box were creeping out again. Jean-Claude began to let the desire to kiss Brad wash over him again. He began playing that memory again of Brad naked and the feelings he had in the ditch. Jean-Claude's chest tightened, he began shaking and tears were coming to his eyes. "What is happening to me?" was all Jean-Claude could think of as he fell asleep crying.

The following week the Battalion moved out to the field for live fire qualifications in Howenfels. This was the first time Jean-Claude would be driving the assigned duce and a half. Or as Sergeant Bird referred to it "the old whore, she might be ugly, but she can get you where you want to go." Sergeant Bird was not too far-off the mark on this truck, it was a left-over from WWII, and Jean-Claude swore it was held together by a little spit and some bubble gum.

> Ms. Wauneta roared with laughter, "The old whore! I didn't know your boss knew me back

then Chickie!" Jean-Claude and Ms. Wauneta fell over laughing at the thought.

The convoy was a nightmare. While traveling in convoys in Germany the US Military must comply with noise levels and speed, especially when driving through towns. Vehicles must remain spaced properly and arranged to comply with noise levels. Jean-Claude often wondered how the Germans dealt with an entire Battalion driving down the cobblestone streets at crack of butt in the morning. Traveling at 35 MPH makes the drive long and boring only stopping for fuel, and vehicle repairs. Sergeant Bird had strapped two tinfoil packages to the motor of the duce and a half before pulling out. Jean-Claude didn't ask what this was for, but when they stopped at the fuel point, Sergeant Bird pulled them off the motor and handed one package to Jean-Claude. Jean-Claude opened it up and there was large piece of fish, carrots, onions, sliced potatoes all perfectly cooked. Jean-Claude's first lesson in engine cooking was complete.

Jean-Claude was so green he didn't know all these rules and about three hours into the drive he had to piss like a racehorse. Jean-Claude started bouncing around in the driver's seat and Sergeant Bird asked, "What is your problem?" "Gotta piss bad," Jean-Claude replied. Sergeant Bird laughed and said, "Remember you asked why I had this empty bottle; well now you know. See that flap on the floor between your feet? Flip it up with your foot and there you go." Jean-Claude looked at Sergeant Bird with a look of shock and said, "You have to be kidding." Sergeant Bird replied, "Your choice, but we are not pulling over for a few more hours." Jean-Claude elected to use the flap, as he opened it up he could see the road below and the brake lines. Keeping his foot on the gas, Sergeant Bird leaning over and steering the truck, Jean-Claude took care of business. "Ah, so much better," Jean-Claude sighed.

"Ewww, you peed on your feet?" Ms. Wauneta asked. "No! Through the hole in the floor under the flap to the road below!" Jean-Claude explained quickly. "Oh, I was gonna say…" her voice trailing off as she was trying to pick out some rouge.

The weather was unusually hot for this time of year in Germany. Jean-Claude woke up in the field the next morning after arrival, stepped outside and he felt like he was going to melt in the brutal humid morning air. The Company First Sergeant was behind Jean-Claude and said, "Well it looks like another hot day today out here." Jean-Claude just made a face at the First Sergeant and headed off to the showers to get ready for the day.

Since this was Jean-Claude's first field exercise he had no idea what was going to happen, but as with most military personnel; they adapt quickly, and this was no exception. Sergeant Bird yelled across the camp, "Jean-Claude get over here, we need to pack up." "Huh? What is this, no one told me we were moving out so soon." he thought. Jean-Claude helped load up the truck and climbed into the front seat to drive the duce and a half to the firing range. If the heat was brutal outside, inside the cabin of the truck was even worse. No breeze was flowing through the truck and the heat from the engine simply added to the discomfort.

After arriving at the firing range, Jean-Claude looked around. It was nothing more than a huge dust bowl with an eight-foot high by twelve-foot wide cement block with stairs next to a travel lane, a Command building and latrines. Jean-Claude had seen outhouses back in Michigan in better shape than these latrines. Jean-Claude thought, "When you have to go, you don't complain. It could be worse, you could be cozying up to a tree with leaves to wipe with and you better know the difference between poison oak and regular leaves." Jean-Claude let out a little laugh of the image of guys running around with the bum itches.

Jean-Claude quickly found out the intended use of the cement block - an Ammo Pad. Jean-Claude quickly set off to unload all the ammo from the truck to the pad and begin counting the rounds into issuable sets for qualifying runs the Bradley teams would be making. Since this was a live fire range, the ammo pad could not be unstaffed while there were live rounds stored on the pad. This proved to be a challenge since Jean-Claude was the only person sanctioned to issue ammo to the Company. Food was brought over to him when Sergeant Bird arrived from camp and he could get off the pad for a bit. Jean-Claude asked Sergeant Bird, "How are we going to work out the sleeping schedule? I haven't sleep since yesterday." Sergeant Bird looked at Jean-Claude with sympathy and replied, "You will not get any sleep until they can pull a duty roster together. Don't fall asleep up here or they will give you an Article 15 and make sure you account for the rounds going out and coming in after each qualifying Bradley team."

Lack of sleep made Jean-Claude crabby. When the Battalion Commander came off the range from his qualification, Jean-Claude ran the rod down the barrel of the turret and felt the rod come to a sudden stop and heard a click. Jean-Claude immediately asked the Battalion Commander, "How many rounds were fired?" The Battalion called for the Gunner and asked the same question. The Gunner looked at the Battalion Commander and Jean-Claude and said, "I'm not sure." "What the Fuck!" Jean-Claude yelled, "Get the fuck out of your vehicle now!" The Battalion Commander looked at Jean-Claude and said, "Do you want to repeat that?" "Sorry, Sir, you need to get out of your vehicle now. I think you have a live round jammed and I have to clear you, but I need to know how many rounds were fired because there might be two rounds jammed together. It might be nice to know before I blow my hand off." Jean-Claude said sarcastically.

Jean-Claude again asked the Gunner, "Seriously, I need you to pull your head out of your ass and figure out the count of rounds fired. If you can't I will shut this range down if you can't come up with a number in the next minute." The Gunner attempted to figure out the count, however, he was too slow and Jean-Claude picked up the radio and closed the range. The Battalion Commander asked, "What do you think you are doing?" Jean-Claude looked at the Battalion Commander and said, "I have the authority to close down the range since your Gunner cannot tell us out of the 56 rounds issued how many were fired. Therefore, I don't know how many rounds are jammed. If one of the rounds were to either cook off or I set it off when I get in there it will go down range where we have personnel on their firing runs. Until I clear everything you can't go any place." Just at that moment the Company Commander pulled up and asked what was closing the range. Jean-Claude explained and asked the Commander to take the Battalion Commander away for a while and when it was cleared the Driver and Gunner would release vehicle.

> "Ooooh, such a man you are; look at you all forceful and what not. Didn't know you had it in your bag of tricks Chickie, you are so quiet and polite when you are around now." Ms. Wauneta smirked at Jean-Claude in the mirror.

After 53 hours into this adventure and no sleep in the near future a PFC walked up to the Ammo Pad and said, "I'm here to guard the pad while you get some sleep." "Thanks, I'll just be here on the cot, just wake me up when you see a Bradley heading our way." Jean-Claude glanced over and simply collapsed on top of the cot. Not even 40 minutes into his sleep Jean-Claude was being woken up by the PFC, there were three Bradley vehicles heading to the Ammo Pad. This continued for seven days and nights. No showers, taking a whore bath (water in a helmet and scrubbing the pits, tits and ass), urinating off the side of the Ammo Pad and sleeping when the chance arose. Jean-Claude felt so dirty from all the grime it was simply a recipe for misery.

Jean-Claude was never happier than to get into camp where he could get into a hot shower. As he was walking towards the showers, Jean-Claude saw Sergeant Dobson wearing a towel around his waist, flip-flops, his M-16 slung over his shoulder and pushing a mop bucket towards the shower. "Hey, Sergeant Dobson, what the hell are you doing?" Jean-Claude yelled out. Sergeant Dobson didn't even look in his direction and replied, "I'm off to do laundry, leave me alone." Jean-Claude thought, "Oh, this is just too good to pass up, I have to see this one." Sergeant Dobson continued into the showers mop bucket and all, turned on the hot water, put his M-16 in the mop bucket and began taking a shower over the bucket. When he had washed up, he began using the mop as a plunger and was washing his clothes. After a good soaping, on the floor his clothes went for the rinse cycle and the M-16 was getting a bath too. Sergeant Dobson looked at Jean-Claude grinning and said, "Hey I have to wash my ass, might was well clean a weapon and do laundry at the same time." Jean-Claude later learned this was a common sight with several of the guys that had served in Vietnam.

After stopping by to visit Brad, Jean-Claude went back to the billets to find a letter from home on his bunk. He dropped his equipment and sat down on the footlocker to read the letter from his stepmother. It was a four-page letter and started out innocuous enough until he hit the top of page two. There it was in writing, "Your uncle committed suicide...there is no sense coming home since we already had the funeral..." Jean-Claude couldn't read any more, he grabbed his rifle and headed for the door running into Sergeant Bird entering. As Jean-Claude passed Sergeant Bird he shoved the letter into Sergeant Bird's chest and just kept going out the door. Jean-Claude needed to be alone so he found the darkest spot he could find and just sat on the ground crying.

When he got back to his bunk, Sergeant Bird and the First Sergeant were waiting for him, "Do you want to go home?" they asked. "No, I just want to go to sleep right now," as Jean-

Claude climbed into the bunk clothes and all. Jean-Claude was woken up by Sergeant Bird kicking the bunk, "Wake up, we need to get going." Jean-Claude rolled out of the bunk and the First Sergeant said, "Ask him, I want to know." Sergeant Bird looked at Jean-Claude and asked, "What day is it?" Jean-Claude replied, "Tuesday afternoon." The First Sergeant and Sgt Bird started laughing hard and said, "No, it is Thursday late morning." Jean-Claude had slept from Monday evening until Thursday. Jean-Claude later found out the First Sergeant had given orders under penalty of 60 days extra duty not to wake Jean-Claude up for any reason.

Jean-Claude would think about the letter and get angry. The thoughts going through his head were: "Where does she get off making the choice for me? She knows all she had to do was call the Red Cross; I told her all that before I left. Fuck, she is such a bitch, this is just another way for her to control. At some point this is going to come back on her." Jean-Claude pushed through his feelings the best he could and kept shoving hard to push them deep inside so he wouldn't have to deal with them any longer.

> "Oh my, what a nasty little woman. Well you can't control what other people do Chickie. They do strange things and it is our duty to figure out how to handle it." Ms. Wauneta said while digging for her lipstick.

A few more weeks of qualifying and it was time to return to garrison. Jean-Claude was in the last convoy out because he was Supply. This time the Amory would be traveling with them fully loaded with every weapon in the Company. Sending the ammo supply ahead in the second convoy since it would not be wise to have ammo and weapons in the same convoy should they be intercepted by anyone.

Everything was going well as they were advancing faster than normal. Because Sergeant Bird had purposely stayed late the convoy wouldn't have to drive under the speed controls since it was made up of five trucks. As they were driving the truck carrying the weapons pulled off to the side of the road and Jean-Claude had to stop and stay with the vehicle. The weapons truck had a flat tire which would need repairing before they could continue. Sergeant Bird ordered the remaining trucks to continue home and the two remaining trucks would catch up when the tire repair was completed.

Jean-Claude and the other truck driver repaired the tire and they were back on the road. They had not even traveled three miles when Jean-Claude heard the pop and felt the truck pull to the side. "Shit, we have a flat now." Jean-Claude stated. Sergeant Bird quickly picked up the radio and called for the weapons truck to pull over. The tire was fixed and again was on their way home. Around 15 miles further, another tire went flat. This time Sergeant Bird told the weapons truck to continue without them and get back to Garrison before it got dark. When Jean-Claude looked at the problem it was the inside tire of the two, "Fuck, now I have to change two tires." Jean-Claude yelled and kicked the tire. Without the help of another driver it was taking much longer to fix the tire this time. The tires were larger than Jean-Claude and wrestling them around took some doing and he learning what not to do more than anything else. Finally, after about 45 minutes Jean-Claude, with the help of Sergeant Bird, figured out how to manipulate the tools to help in changing these massive tires.

Back on the road again…not much further and another flat tire. This continued the entire trip. A duce and a half has ten tires, so far eight of them had gone flat on this trip and it was getting later and later. They were about five miles from garrison when Jean-Claude felt the pull of the wheel again. He looked at Sergeant Bird wearily and said, "We have another flat, it is on your side can you look out the window and tell me which tire it is?" Sergeant Bird leaned out the side of the truck and replied, "It is the front axle inside." Jean-Claude looked at Sergeant Bird,

"Oh hell no! We are so close, that tire can peel off on the road for all I care, but I'm not changing another tire! I will pay for it if it is damaged." They went thumping down the road towards home.

Jean-Claude glanced down at his watch as they were pulling into the Kaserne, "Fuck, it is 0230 in the morning, we are going to piss people off tonight Sergeant Bird." "Yep, but hey we made it. What time did we start Mr. Toad's Wild Ride?" he said chuckling. Jean-Claude started figuring it out; they had been on the road for 18 hours. Jean-Claude would receive his first medal for his efforts on this field exercise.

The next weekend after returning to garrison, Brad and Jean-Claude went out to party to let off some steam. They went to the bowling alley, had some beers and played a couple of games. Then back to Brad's barracks to drink some more and hang out. Brad and Jean-Claude could talk about almost anything; but Jean-Claude never dared mention he had the hots for Brad. When it was time to go to bed, Brad sacked out in his bunk and Jean-Claude fell asleep on the couch directly across from Brad's bunk. Jean-Claude woke up in the middle of the night and looked at Brad sleeping without any covers over his body. Brad was wearing bikini shorts and was sporting a huge bulge. Jean-Claude couldn't get back to sleep, he just lay there gazing on Brad's hot body and thinking of all the sexual things that they could do together.

The next weekend the guys from HQ Platoon came to Jean-Claude and said, "You are going with us to Frankfurt as it is tradition that we take the new guy out for the night." Jean-Claude replied, "Cool, I will be there." Saturday evening Jean-Claude and five other guys caught the train to Frankfurt, but they refused to tell Jean-Claude what was in store for him that evening. When they hit the streets of Frankfurt they all stopped at the first bar they came along for a drink. It was Jean-Claude's task to drink a beer and a shot at each bar they stopped along the way. Jean-

Claude thought, "I hope we don't stop a lot 'cause I will not make it!"

After the third bar, the guys turned down a side street and Jean-Claude saw all the red lights lining the street. The guys looked at Jean-Claude to see his reaction as they kept walking. Everywhere Jean-Claude turned there were women in windows, doorways and barkers inviting guys into the establishments. It didn't take long for Jean-Claude to figure out these were working women. The guys turned into a nondescript building and Jean-Claude just followed. Up the stairs they went looking in all the open rooms and they finally stopped in front of one. "Hey, Jean-Claude what do you think of this one?" Jean-Claude took a look and said, "Very nice." "Good, get in there," as they shoved him into the room closing the door behind Jean-Claude.

Jean-Claude stood there looking at the woman who was putting on her lipstick in the mirror, she looked at him in the mirror and said, "Sit down honey." Jean-Claude walked over to the bed and sat down on the very edge. The woman came over and sat down next to Jean-Claude and spoke quietly, "Just relax, I know you are not interested. We can just sit here and talk and when the time is up we will just open the door and your friends won't know the difference." Jean-Claude just looked at her; he didn't know what she meant. It wasn't that he wasn't interested; he just had never had sex with anyone.

The woman continued, "You know, I know a place that you can go that you would be more comfortable." She got up and reached in the dresser and brought out a business card with just an address on it and handed it to Jean-Claude. "Trust me honey, you will have a good time here when you are ready, but only go when you are ready." Jean-Claude just sat there looking at here not knowing what to say or what exactly she meant by "when you are ready." "Ready for what?" he thought. The woman sat back down and they had a conversation about her business. Jean-Claude found out she was married, her husband didn't mind at all that she slept with guys for money because she made more than he did and she only worked eight months of the year. It was legal to be a prostitute in Germany; they tested every week for STDs and HIV.

The woman stood up and said, "Ok honey, time is up. I'll give you a few minutes to collect yourself and then let me open the door." Jean-Claude just nodded not saying a word. When she opened the door Jean-Claude walked towards it listening to the hoots and hollers of the guys waiting outside the door. All of them assumed Jean-Claude had just slept with the prostitute; and he was happy to let them think whatever they wanted.

"Hey wait, I thought you had sex with a woman, not her?" Ms. Wauneta inquired. "No, that is coming, don't get your panties in a twist." Jean-Claude replied. "HA! Get my panties in a twist. Honey, my panties have not been twisted in such a long time; I'm not sure what I would do if that happened." Ms. Wauneta pulled the goo off her eyelash adhesive.

Jean-Claude continued learning from Sergeant Bird and taking on more responsibility as time went along. Fewer than 30 days after returning from weapons qualifications there was a General Inspection. After three weeks of working 18 hour days to prepare for the inspection began to take a toll on Jean-Claude. Sergeant Bird and Jean-Claude looked like the walking dead during the inspection. As Sergeant Bird said, "There is time for sleep once this thing is over, and we must get top scores on this inspection so they leave us alone." Needless to say, all the hard work paid off.

After inspection, Jean-Claude left on a pass to England for five days. It was a great deal, five days, four nights, all transportation and a four-star hotel with two meals a day for $68.00 US. No passport was required considering Military ID was a passport. Jean-Claude went with Carol who he had met several months prior. Jean-Claude and Carol had slept together one time before this trip and Jean-Claude was repulsed at the thought of having sex with a woman from that one experience. Before having sex with Carol, Jean-Claude was a virgin. However, Jean-Claude thought, "Maybe it is not that bad, maybe you just have to get use to it." So he set off to have sex again with Carol while they were on this trip.

On the second night of the trip, Carol and Jean-Claude had sex; it was a disaster. Jean-Claude couldn't continue and was just simply grossed out at the thought of continuing. Carol thought it was her fault, since she was just as inexperienced and was a virgin as well.

A couple of nights passed after returning from the London trip and Jean-Claude finally went to see Carol and broke up with her. Jean-Claude trying all the classics: "it's not you, it's me" statements, but it didn't help; Carol was distraught and there was no consoling her.

> "Oh Chickie, I'm sorry you had to go through that. But at some point I think most of us queens go through that stage of let me sleep with a woman and maybe I won't be attracted to men." Ms. Wauneta said while patting her face with powder sending a dust cloud up into the air.

Todd

It was almost two weeks after Jean-Claude's break-up with Carol that Todd introduced himself to Jean-Claude. Todd was also from the 26th Support Battalion. Todd was 5'10", slender, about 135 pounds, brown hair, brown eyes and a beautiful smile with smooth olive skin. Todd had lips that were just made for kissing as Jean-Claude would soon find out. It was a Friday night when Jean-Claude met him, and both he and Todd were into video games, Jean-Claude invited him back to his office in Alpha Company to play a video game. It never crossed Jean-Claude's mind Todd had something else in mind though.

After about an hour of playing the video game, Jean-Claude heard a voice down the hall, it was Carol speaking with the Company CQ. The office door was closed, so she didn't know that he was in the office. The phone rang, "hello?" Jean-Claude said into the phone. "There is a woman here to speak with you" said the CQ. Jean-Claude replied, "Yes, I heard her, I'll be right there."

Jean-Claude walked down the hall and took Carol by the arm and led her down the stairs towards the front door. He explained to her, "I don't want to see you and it would be best if we didn't see each other right now, we both need our space." Carol was angry and replied, "You fucked me and that was all you wanted, what kind of person do you think I am." Jean-Claude had no idea how to reply and said the only thing that came to his mind, "Maybe you should just go and we will talk later." With that he turned and left her standing outside the front door of Alpha Company.

Heading back up the stairs Jean-Claude thought, "This is going to get worse, I just have a feeling." Jean-Claude headed into the office and sat back down where he and Todd went back to playing the video game. After about 30 minutes of playing the game, Todd put his hand on Jean-Claude's leg; Jean-Claude didn't move, he liked Todd touching him and Jean-Claude put his hand on Todd's arm.

As Todd leaned over Jean-Claude to look at the screen he turned and kissed Jean-Claude. Jean-Claude's entire body began to shake nervously and his skin was tingling. Then Todd placed his hand on Jean-Claude's crotch where Jean-Claude was hard as rock with excitement of what might happen.

Just as Todd and Jean-Claude were getting passionate with the kissing, there was a shrill scream from outside the window, it was Carol. She said, "I know who you are up there with and I know what you are doing with him too, everyone knows about him." Jean-Claude chose to ignore her and she would eventually go away. After about 20 minutes of screaming at a window that was never going to open, she gave up and went back to her barracks.

Jean-Claude and Todd just keep looking at each other and went back to the foreplay that had started earlier as if nothing had happened. For Jean-Claude this was a new experience and he was not going to let anything stand in his way of this adventure. Todd and Jean-Claude moved over to the floor pulling down some blankets off the shelf and they began having oral sex right in the office.

After they were both spent, they both got dressed and Todd said, "Thanks, I need to get going, see you later." Jean-Claude looked at him and just nodded and walked towards the door. Jean-Claude walked Todd downstairs and out the front door and watched as he walked away. Jean-Claude was confused over having an exciting evening with a guy and it felt good. "What is going on with me?" he thought.

> "Oh my, Chickie that really wasn't a 'first time' experience you know. It was just experimentation. A 'first time' experience is when you just want to lose yourself in the other person, otherwise it is just goofing around." Ms. Wauneta glanced over at Jean-Claude. "Yes, I know, I'm getting there." Jean-Claude replied.

Jean-Claude went to bed feeling light-headed and excited; he liked having sex with a guy. It was so much better and fun than being with a woman. Jean-Claude woke up the next morning still feeling the aftereffects of the night prior. Jean-Claude lived with three straight guys. Gensler a short 5'5", 140 pound jerk that was the Commander's driver. Hunter, a 5'11", 150 pound, brown hair, green-eyed quiet guy who was in charge of the armory. Pickard who was assigned to our room from First Platoon who was primarily ignored.

Gensler started in with "so what's this about you being a fag?" Jean-Claude was surprised and said, "What are you talking about?" "We are talking about the chick yelling at the window saying you were gay dude." Jean-Claude thought quickly, "control the information, NOW!" and said, "Oh she is just pissed because I broke up with her and she didn't like it." Gensler looked at Jean-Claude and smirked as he said, "Yeah, broads they don't get it do they."

Jean-Claude had broken out in a full cold sweat with this conversation. "Shit, what is going to happen now? Does everyone know what Todd and I were doing? Shit, shit, shit" was all he could think while dodging off to the shower. When he finished his shower, Jean-Claude shot out the door and over to 26th Support Battalion, he had to see Todd and let him know what was said. Jean-Claude stopped at the CQ desk and asked for Todd and the PFC behind the desk looked him up and down while telling him Todd's room number. As Jean-Claude was walking up the stairs he heard the PFC say to the Sergeant, "There goes another one of them." Jean-Claude wasn't sure what he meant exactly, but he had a pretty good idea.

Knocking on Todd's door, Jean-Claude was shaking as he heard the lock being turned and Todd's face poked around the door. "I have to talk to you now." Jean-Claude said to Todd; Todd opened the door and said, "Get in here, I need to get dressed and we can go eat." Todd was in his boxers, and Jean-Claude just stared at him getting ready thinking about having sex with him again, forgetting what he needed to talk to Todd about.

After dressing Todd headed off to the mess hall together and Jean-Claude advised Todd about what was said about being a fag. Todd said, "Don't worry about it, they can say anything they want to say, but if they cannot prove it they can't throw you out of the Army." "Won't they investigate just from this?" Jean-

Claude asked. Todd laughed, "No, now stop worrying and have fun." After breakfast, Jean-Claude headed to Todd's room and they had sex again.

> "Chickie, I bet you didn't know this but I was in the Navy a long time ago. Your friend Todd was correct. For the most part if you did your job and stayed under the radar everyone in command would leave you alone." Ms. Wauneta clucked and turned her head back and forth looking at her artwork in the mirror.

Jean-Claude would run into Todd every once in awhile around the Kaserne, but Todd would keep his distance. It was more of a relationship of convenience for both men; whenever they wanted sex, they knew where to go to get it.

The next weekend, Jean-Claude went and hung out with the guys from Alpha Company bouncing from bar to bar on Friday night. He figured if he hung out with them for a bit and played 'cover up' they would get off his back and not question if he was straight. That night they drank so much that Jean-Claude blacked out and, when he woke up on Sunday, had no recollection of late Friday night to Sunday.

Brad and Jean-Claude were back to hanging out all the time; goofing around and drinking a lot of the time they were together. Drinking would often lead to wrestling with each other, even though Brad was stronger than Jean-Claude he could never fully pin Jean-Claude down. Jean-Claude looked forward to these wrestling sessions because he was able to feel Brad's hard sexy body next to his. Every once in awhile, Jean-Claude would grab Brad's crotch while wrestling and what a crotch it was too.

One night it was late and both Brad and Jean-Claude were tired and wanted to just watch a movie so they went over to Jean-Claude's room. At this time, Jean-Claude had obtained a single room in Alpha Company so having a guest was no problem. After watching the movie, Jean-Claude fell asleep on the floor and Brad in the bed. Jean-Claude kept waking up throughout the night, looking at Brad, wanting to get into the bed with him and lie next to him.

As with all military personnel, it was Brad's turn to return to the States and he asked if Jean-Claude could give him a ride to the airport to catch his flight. Jean-Claude cleared it with Sergeant Bird and approval was given so long as Jean-Claude returned in time to catch the trucks out to Grafenwohr.

On the appointed day, Jean-Claude went over to Delta Company to see if Brad was ready and the CQ advised that Brad was still in the shower. Jean-Claude went into the shower area to see what the holdup was because it was past the time that they should have left. Brad was just finishing his shower and turned to looked at Jean-Claude and said, "Give me a few and I'll be ready." Jean-Claude just stared at Brad's hot naked body not really registering what Brad had just said. Jean-Claude had often fantasized about seeing Brad fully naked and this was better than anything he ever imagined. The crotch that Jean-Claude had grazed several times while wrestling with Brad was huge. Brad's well-defined chest, legs and ass were on full display as well. Jean-Claude had to get out of there as he was getting hard at the site of Brad in the shower. Jean-Claude would forever have this image of Brad for future reference.

Brad and Jean-Claude headed off to Rheine-Mein Airport to catch the plane. They arrived early, decided to have breakfast together and relax since it was going to be about an hour before the flight. They hung out like two brothers that had grown up together, joking, poking fun and talking about the future. Then the announcement came over the speakers and it was time for Brad to head to the departure gate. Brad came over to Jean-Claude, gave him a huge hug and said, "Take care of yourself and I'll write to you when I'm settled."

Jean-Claude didn't watch Brad leave; he quickly turned and started back to the car as he needed to get back home in time to catch the convoy headed out to the field. Jean-Claude started to drive on the autobahn but within 15 minutes had to pull off the road and stop because he could no longer see through the tears. Jean-Claude was sobbing uncontrollably as feeling alone washed over him and his love for Brad took over. He never told Brad how he really felt because he was too afraid of losing him. There was a large void in Jean-Claude's heart as he thought of Brad. When he got back to Graves Kaserne he hopped out of the car and into the back of the truck heading out. Jean-Claude cried the entire four hour trip, in the back of the truck alone.

"See I told you; your first man-crush!" Ms. Wauneta gleefully exclaimed. "Oh be quiet over there." Jean-Claude said teasingly. "I think we all fall for some hot straight friend that we have at some point or another. That is just part of life you know." Ms. Wauneta said poking Jean-Claude in the side.

Jean-Claude had always felt alone, even growing up and here he was again, alone missing the hell out of Brad. Jean-Claude thought, "Why does anyone that means anything to me go away?" Jean-Claude finally began distracting himself with work and carried on through the field exercise.

When Alpha Company returned home, there were people waiting for the returning soldiers; Jean-Claude looked around and there was no one, not even Todd. Jean-Claude thought, "I at least thought Todd might show up, oh well." Jean-Claude hauled his bags out of the truck and up to his room. After dropping them in the corner and he went down to the truck waiting for the detail that would be helping move the ammunition crates from the truck back to the vault in the basement. This was the worst part of returning from the field, putting everything back and washing all the equipment down —no one wanted to be there; they all wanted to go home and rest.

From behind Jean-Claude a deep smooth voice said, "Are you Jean-Claude?" Jean-Claude about jumped out of his skin because he was not expecting anyone this soon and he turned and said, "Yes." "I'm Lance, nice to meet you, I was told to meet you here to help." Lance replied with a smile. Jean-Claude looked surprised, Lance was a black man, 6'1", 185 pounds, medium firm build with long arms and legs, and a perfect smile.

> "Oh honey, some chocolate! Hmm, I didn't know you had it in your disposition Chickie." Ms. Wauneta exclaimed while bouncing up and down on her seat. "Calm down over there, it doesn't end well." Jean-Claude frowned at her.

Jean-Claude explained what they would be doing once the other guys showed up. Meanwhile they just needed to wait because it required at least three guys to unload the truck for security reasons. Lance was asking Jean-Claude about Alpha Company and what it was like. Jean-Claude finally figured it out; Lance had arrived from the States when they were out in the field, no wonder he was so curious. Jean-Claude was tired and would have normally been snippy but there was something about this guy. Lance mentioned to Jean-Claude that his wife would not be joining him over here and it was going to be a long duty assignment. "Hmm, what is he saying?" Jean-Claude thought.

Lance

Finally the other guys showed up and they started to unload the truck. Lance stayed close to Jean-Claude during the task. Jean-Claude thought it a little odd, but didn't give it much thought. As Jean-Claude was locking up the vault, Lance said, "Do you want to hang out tomorrow afternoon?" "Sure" said Jean-Claude, "Why don't you come down to my room and we can watch TV and relax." Lance agreed and he gave Jean-Claude a pat on the back and let his hand linger longer than normal.

Jean-Claude thought, "That is strange, wonder what is up with that?"

The next day, Lance knocked on the door and Jean-Claude let him into his room. They hung out watching TV and talking about a bunch of things; but Lance kept touching Jean-Claude either on the leg or his arm. Stimulated from this touching Jean-Claude he kept the conversation flowing and away from anything too personal about himself.

It was nearing dinner and Lance needed to go upstairs to his room to get a jacket, Jean-Claude followed so they could just leave from Lance's room. After entering the room, Lance turned around and locked the door. As Jean-Claude was turning towards the door, Lance grabbed him up into his arms and kissed him on the lips. Jean-Claude pulled away in surprise, but then went back for more. They immediately went to the bed and began sucking on each other. After both had an orgasm they cleaned up and headed off to dinner, not a single word was said between them about the incident.

A few weeks later, Lance came around again and asked Jean-Claude to "take care of him." Jean-Claude obliged and performed oral sex on Lance. This became a routine and was happening regularly. Jean-Claude began to feel bad about himself in performing like a trained seal for Lance. Jean-Claude couldn't end it because it would be too risky since Lance could turn him in for being gay and they would have believed him since Lance was married. Jean-Claude felt trapped and needed to figure a way out.

One night while on CQ Jean-Claude was making the rounds through the barracks ensure doors were secured when out from the stairwell Brown walked out. Grabbing Jean-Claude by the back of the neck and quietly said in his ear, "Come with me, we know what you have been doing for Lance." Jean-Claude was scared; he didn't know what was waiting for him as he was pushed up the stairs. Brown was huge, he was 6'2", a chest as wide as a wall locker, just massive, there was no escaping this either. When they reached the top of the stairs Brown told Jean-Claude to open the storage room. Since Jean-Claude always carried the keys on him, he opened the door. Brown pushed Jean-Claude inside and closed the door. In the dim light, Jean-Claude could see Brown grinning at him. Brown reached down and grabbed Jean-Claude's hand and put it to his crotch and held it there against his hard cock. Jean-Claude knew what was coming next and prepared himself. Brown said, "Yeah, we know you like dick and will suck cock if asked so get to work on it." Jean-Claude fell to his knees and pulled out Brown's hard cock. Jean-Claude stifled a laugh before he took Brown into his mouth, Jean-Claude was thinking, "Wow, for such a big buff man he sure has a tiny dick." After Brown had unloaded into Jean-Claude's mouth he simply turned and left the storage room. Jean-Claude quickly locked up and headed back to the CQ desk. The duty sergeant never said a word to him about his prolonged absence. Soon after that, the comments started; guys were calling him a fag.

> Ms. Wauneta put her makeup brush down on the table and said, "How horrible, you warned me that it didn't end well, you were right. Jean-Claude just nodded agreeing.

For the next few weeks Jean-Claude was a real ass to everyone. Since he carried the Gideon for the Company and he ran in formation right behind the Commander, Jean-Claude would encourage the Commander to take long grueling runs making sure to suggest steep hills. As these runs became a regular part of PT, Jean-Claude was laughing to himself, "Now let's see what these assholes do now." Jean-Claude knew what it was doing to the guys running behind him and he enjoyed being the cause of their pain.

However; one time he must have said something just loud enough for the first squad to hear him and one of the guys hissed, "You're dead meat Jean-Claude." Jean-Claude didn't give it much thought and just kept running. The next evening Jean-Claude had to work late finishing paperwork for a trip to the depot the next day when the office door swung open revealing Lance, Brown and Clark. They all entered the office and shut the door throwing the lock as they progressed around the desk towards Jean-Claude. Obviously the guy in the first squad told them what he was doing and they were here to make sure it didn't happen again. Brown did the talking for the three of them. "If you ever do something as stupid as that again we will fuck you up literally. Think about what I'm saying because we will start with Clark shoving that big cock of his up your ass boy." Jean-Claude was scared; he had gone too far this time. Brown turned to Lance and Clark saying, "You guys can leave, I'm going to give him a taste of what might happen." Lance and Clark left the room; Brown locked the door behind them while saying, "Get over here and suck my dick." Jean-Claude got in front of Brown and sucked on him for about ten minutes when Brown pulled Jean-Claude's head off his cock and ordered, "Stand up and bend over I want to fuck that ass." Brown was pulling off Jean-Claude's BDUs and bending him over. Brown tried to shove his little dick inside Jean-Claude but Jean-Claude was fast and scooted away pulling up his pants. Turning to Brown Jean-Claude said, "Really this is what you want to do? Trust me, if you ever lay a finger on me or open your mouth or even look at me funny you will regret ever meeting me." Jean-Claude was laying the groundwork for thermonuclear warfare. Jean-Claude made the determination that he would get the upper hand and keep it that way. Brown backed away from Jean-Claude as Jean-Claude unlocked the door and opened it. Jean-Claude hissed, "Get out before I raise my voice and you regret ever stepping foot on this earth." Brown hurried out the door and down the hallway. When Jean-Claude would get angry he would become quiet, this was the most dangerous time because Jean-Claude was contemplating how he would retaliate.

Jean-Claude slammed the door shut and locked it. "Who in the fuck do they think they are playing with? Don't they know that I can really fuck them up? Stupid grunts," he said out loud. Jean-Claude went back to the paperwork and began stewing over what had happened and made plans to get all three of them back soon.

The day of reckoning was on Brown, Lance and Clark; Jean-Claude had chosen the exact date and time it was going to happen. Again, since Jean-Claude carried the Company Gideon he had access to the First Sergeant every morning at first call. While they were standing waiting for reports from the platoons, Jean-Claude quietly said, "Top, we need to talk about Brown, Lance and Clark and what they did last week in my office." Top replied, "I heard there was something going on late at night, but figured you would let me know if there was a problem. So tell me quickly what happened." Jean-Claude said, "They burst into the office, threatened me because I was urging the Commander to take them on long runs and they didn't like it." Top asked, "Was it bodily harm?" "Yes," Jean-Claude replied.

Without a second thought the First Sergeant called out, "Brown, Lance and Clark, report." All three guys came running up behind Jean-Claude; standing at attention. First Sergeant asked, "Did the three of you enter the supply office after hours last week?" All three guys replied with a "Yes, First Sergeant." "That is fine, go wait in my office," was the reply from the First Sergeant. Jean-Claude knew what was going to happen to the three of them, an Article 15 was going to be issued against them and they were going to get extra duty hours. Jean-Claude thought, "Step one is complete, now on to step two."

Jean-Claude had been holding onto the information that Battalion S-4 had sought he transfer up as quickly as possible, but Jean-Claude had asked that they hold off on the request until after the field exercise. Jean-Claude was about to accelerate these plans to get out of Alpha Company and away from the three guys he just set up.

Later that morning, Jean-Claude visited the S-4 officer and it was agreed the transfer would happen immediately. The orders issued by early afternoon. After lunch Jean-Claude was in the office when the Commander came around the corner steaming, "What the hell is this with you moving immediately up to S-4?" Jean-Claude playing dumb replied, "They requested it happen, who am I to question orders?" "Well I need a driver and a vehicle for the field exercise if you are going any place" the Commander demanded. Jean-Claude was already ahead of him and replied, "You will have a 5-ton truck with a driver from HHQ Company at your disposal for the entire duration of the field exercise." The Commander looked surprised and said, "How did you know I was going to ask for that?" Jean-Claude replied, "That is part of my job to anticipate the needs of a Company and you forget that at Battalion I control the motor pool." The Commander just glared at Jean-Claude and said, "Start moving your stuff this afternoon."

Jean-Claude could be extremely cold and calculating when he needed to be under the guise of self-preservation. He could have easily stayed in Alpha Company until after the field exercise without any problems, but he simply wanted away from all of them. Jean-Claude quickly began the process of moving out of Alpha Company and moving across the Kaserne to HHQ on top of the hill.

"Well, remind me not to piss you off!" Ms. Wauneta said as she tossed a used cotton ball in Jean-Claude's direction. "It's those quiet ones you always have to worry about now isn't it?"

HHQ – Battalion S-4

Jean-Claude moved into a four-person room with Small a driver assigned to Battalion S-4, Griggs who was the Battalion

Legal Clerk, and Benson who was the Battalion Intelligence Clerk. Jean-Claude outranked everyone in the room both by hard grade and position at Battalion. Jean-Claude was to replace the Battalion Supply Sergeant who was getting ready to transition and there was no one to fill the slot since there was a shortage of supply personnel.

Jean-Claude knew who all the members of S-4 were since he had worked with them all in the past. However, this was going to be different since he was brought into S-4 to take a leadership role in S-4. Jean-Claude had just arrived in his new office and the Command Sergeant Major (CSM) was asking to see him in his office. All interactions with the CSM before this day didn't go well and Jean-Claude was not looking forward to his meeting with the CSM.

Jean-Claude entered the CSM's office the CSM said, "I know how you got up here and I don't like it, stay out of my way and we will get along, I'm leaving in a couple of months anyway. You will need to prepare for a Change of Command accountability inspection immediately." Jean-Claude ask, "Why so soon?" CSM replied, you are the new Battalion S-4, you will need to account for every piece of equipment in the Battalion and sign for it from the current Battalion S-4 NCO." Jean-Claude replied, "Yes CSM." "Dismissed" said the CSM.

As Jean-Claude was walking back to his office he sighed a bit and thought, "Well that wasn't too bad." When Jean-Claude entered the S-4 office the outgoing S-4 NCO said, "Hi, this will be your desk" as he stood up and came around to the front. Continuing, "You will begin taking over immediately since I only have 30 days left in country and need to start clearing." Jean-Claude thought, "well shit, no rest for the weary, I guess we will hit the ground running." The door to S-4 opened and Captain Ryan, the Battalion S-4 officer poked his head in and said, "I need to see both of you right now." Into the Captain's office we went. Captain Ryan started off with, "Hope you are settling in, we need to start planning for a field exercise that has been moved up to the beginning of next month. We are taking another Battalion's slot in the field for rotation." The outgoing NCO said, "That is all his, I will be clearing." Jean-Claude just looked and said, "Yes, Sir."

"Shit, fuck, damn, they didn't tell me all these things. Now how the hell are we suppose to do inventory count and prepare for a large scale field exercise at the same time and be ready to leave on time?" Jean-Claude was mulling it over in his head. Jean-Claude settled down and the outgoing NCO started explaining his system of the office. Jean-Claude listened halfheartedly since he knew he was going to change things anyway. The current Battalion S-4 was notorious for not doing anything and was about as useful as tits on a boar. Jean-Claude had been tasked to fix this problem when he was selected to move to S-4.

The next day Jean-Claude called a shop meeting and advised the shop personnel what was coming down the pike. What the assignments would be for the inventory inspection as well as planning to move out to the field by the end of the month. Immediately two of the soldiers started bitching. Jean-Claude nipped that in the bud real fast by saying, "If you have an issue with it I will be more than happy to transfer you back to a unit this afternoon and find someone else to do your job." Dead silence. "Now you have your assignments, let's just get through this and we will figure things out along the way." Jean-Claude said and sat down and started to work. He heard some complaining as they were leaving the shop, but he didn't care. He had a job to do and if they wanted to bitch he would get rid of them, he didn't have time to deal with babies and this was a good assignment for the guys who had transferred up. No soldier at Battalion would want to go back to a unit after all the perks they get with this job.

Jean-Claude went upstairs to S-3 to see his mentor Sergeant Dobson from Alpha Company; they both had been transferred at the same time. As he walked in the door he heard a familiar booming voice, "Hey there Apple head Captain Crunch eating mother fucker, what are you doing in my neck of the woods?" Jean-Claude laughed at Sergeant Dobson because that is how they met the first time at Alpha Company. Jean-Claude was in the supply office eating out of a box of Captain Crunch and working on his personal Apple computer. Sergeant Dobson had entered, "What you eating? Give me some….hmm, what's this thing with all the buttons?" as he proceeded to poke at the keyboard messing up the work Jean-Claude was doing. "Knock it off and get your fingers off the keyboard Sergeant" Jean-Claude exclaimed swatting at the sergeant's hand.

> "HA HA! Apple head you do look the part of the geek you know Jean-Claude, and you are always on your computers doing something." Ms. Wauneta grinned and waived her coffee cup at Jean-Claude, "Be a dear and get mommy some more please."

Jean-Claude held Sergeant Dobson in high regard and would take his advice no questions asked. Jean-Claude started, "Well I've got a couple of problems right out the gate. The outgoing S-4 NCO has pretty much checked himself out and throws his hands up if I ask questions. We are going to have a full inventory accounting for the Battalion within 15 days and, as you know, we have moved up the large field problem now 30 days away. We need to perform both of them and I need some help in planning. And don't get me started on the staff issues that are brewing." Sergeant Dobson chuckled, "Well you go down to that desk of yours and look in the drawers for that Captain Crunch. I know you have some hidden in there and come back up and we will see what we can do to help." Jean-Claude rolled his eyes as he knew he would have to buy another box of cereal, but it was a small price to pay.

Sergeant Dobson and Jean-Claude worked late into the night planning and setting schedules for each company to be issued first thing in the morning. Jean-Claude was exhausted and went up to his new room around 0300. The alarm went off at 0430 as Jean-Claude rolled over he thought, "God, this is going to be a very long day." After PT Jean-Claude went to the office and began making calls to each Company CQ to schedule a meeting with all the Supply Sergeants in the afternoon.

At the afternoon meeting, Jean-Claude advised the Supply Sergeants of the planned schedule to accomplish both the inventory and the prep for field duty. Everyone understood the pressure and Sergeant Bird said, "Well better you than us, you are younger and can handle the stress; just so you know; we all turned the job down and recommended you." Everyone was laughing, Jean-Claude thought, "So this is how he got offered the job...makes sense now, why would an E-4 be filling an E-6 slot?"

The next 30 days were a blur, everything accomplished and everyone worked together to make things happen. The guys in the shop were no worse for wear from getting their butts chewed regularly for nonperformance to the standards Jean-Claude had set. When inventory accounting was finished, Jean-Claude signed for millions of dollars worth of equipment and then the process of issuing it down from Jean-Claude to the Company Supply Sergeants began. For missing items, forms were completed to take it out of the individual's pay that had lost the item. The Army can put any bean counter to shame just getting out of bed. That is mainly what supply does, they are extremely good at counting things, especially if they take their boots off they can get as high as twenty.

The S-4 had two vehicles assigned to it permanently the APC track which was a hand-me-down from Echo Company and a Humvee. On a request/roaming basis S-4 had access to the Battalion VW van and could get trucks with drivers if needed.

It was time for the Battalion to move out to the field. Jean-Claude was in a truck following the S-4 officer in the long convoy traveling no more than 35 MPH. The convoy started at 0730 and finished getting to Howenfels around 2030. Luckily the advance party had gotten everything taken care of and as vehicles rolled into camp they were directed to the motor pool, billeting and the mess hall. Jean-Claude couldn't wait to sleep, just a few hours is all he wanted.

Two days after arriving in base camp it was time to move out and play war games for ten days. Jean-Claude hopped aboard the APC, strapped in and began radio checks while the driver was moving out of the motor pool to join the Battalion convoy to the next stop. After being bounced around inside the APC for about 30 minutes the vehicle finally stopped and dropped open the back door. They were in the woods setting up in a horseshoe formation and the work had to begin. Assignments would be handed out, guard schedules set up, guard posts identified, passwords issued, radios monitored always and coordination with other Battalion groups was just the beginning. Jean-Claude headed over to the S-3 track to get the updated maps that were forgotten by the Lieutenant prior to leaving. Jean-Claude was grousing to himself, "What an idiot, what if we had broken down, how did he expect to find this location without friggin' maps?" Jean-Claude entered the S-3 vehicle and his friend Sergeant Dobson was there with a grin on his face, "Did you forget something before you left?" as he was holding out a set of maps. "Don't say anything, this is going to be a messed up exercise if this is how it is starting with that silly Lieutenant of mine." Sergeant Dobson laughed and said, "I'll check in on you later."

Jean-Claude had been gone about 15 minutes and on his return he learned the Lieutenant had lent the APC driver to Echo Company. "What the fuck is he thinking?" Jean-Claude angrily thought. "Now we are shorthanded and even worse, if we have to pull out, we don't have a driver and are stuck here. What a complete idiot." Jean-Claude got the maps up on the boards with the correct overlays and began setting up the daily reporting with each Company Clerk.

A few hours later Sergeant Dobson showed up at S-4 with the duty roster. "You are not going to like this one bit, your Lieutenant sold you out and you are losing all but one of your guys to the duty roster." Jean-Claude exploded yelling, "Where is that fuckhead? I swear I'm going to kill him." Captain Ryan was coming around the corner and said, "What's up?" Jean-Claude took a breath and advised the Captain what had occurred and finished by saying, "Just keep him away from me, I know he is just here until he gets transferred, but he is killing us here." Captain Ryan agreed to find an assignment away from the S-4 group for the Lieutenant.

Because all of Jean-Claude's assigned soldiers had been pulled he had to figure out how he was going to run S-4 by himself with band aids along the way from whomever he could wrangle to get help. Jean-Claude sat down in front of the radios and the field exercise was in full swing.

On the third day of the exercise the CSM stopped by to check on everything. The CSM was happy to report everything is running smoothly out in the field as far as supply and this was the best they had ever seen the supply chain. Jean-Claude was looking at the CSM in a daze partly because he couldn't hear him over the radio chatter with Jean-Claude having two sets of headphones on his head listening to both radios at the same time. CSM asked, "When was the last time you got any sleep?" Jean-Claude replied, "Not sure, I know I've replaced five sets of plans with overlays. They just bring me coffee and food and we are managing to keep things going." The CSM's eyes got big as he pointed out, "You have been up four days straight? So that is why the Colonel asked me to stop by and check on you, he kept hearing only your voice on the radio."

Jean-Claude was grateful the CSM had stopped by and he had pulled one of the medics to oversee the radios while Jean-Claude slept in the APC sitting in the chair. The medic woke Jean-Claude four hours later saying, "You have to hear this" handing the headset over. Jean-Claude grabbed the headset and was listening to the shouts over the radio. He didn't recognize any of the call signs; grabbing the codebook to check the codes and the radio frequency. "Ah, I see the problem, 'wrong frequency' the medic must not have changed over and S-4 was now picking up a different group" he said to himself. Jean-Claude got up changed the frequency, handed the headset back to the medic and went back to sleep.

Jean-Claude woke up to Sergeant Dobson shaking him, "Hey, hey, time to get up sleeping beauty and let me say you are not any prettier than when you went to sleep." "Oh shut up Sergeant Dobson," Jean-Claude replied, "What's up?" "Nothing much, we just need the medic back, we are a little short over there after we sent some out to the front" Sergeant Dobson said with a smile. Jean-Claude smelled a skunk and asked, "So who's idea was it to short out the medics?" Sergeant Dobson smiled and replied when he saw the look of surprise on Jean-Claude's face, "I'll give you one guess." "Oh God, no" Jean-Claude groaned. "Yep, your Captain Ryan thought it might be a good place to put the Lieutenant in S-3, how much trouble could he cause there right?" laughing Sergeant Dobson grinned from ear to ear "What are you going to do he has to take up space somewhere." Jean-Claude grumbled, "Why not in a hole in the middle of the forest someplace without a map to find us."

Once they finally made it back to camp it was off for a nice long hot shower. Jean-Claude finally got everything settled and put away and headed off to the showers thinking, "I hope there is still some hot water in there." As Jean-Claude entered the shower building walking in facing a long row of sinks and four long rows of toilets, off to the left through another door was the gym-like shower in an open bay. While Jean-Claude was sitting on the bench getting undressed, Rick from the communications group came over asking, "Do you know what time chow is going to be served tonight?" while stuffing his large cock into his tighty-whites. Jean-Claude couldn't help but look at that big cock since he had a thing for Rick from when they were on the same bowling team earlier in the year. Rick saw Jean-Claude looking at his now packed pouch of his underwear and smiled and simply waited for the answer to his question. Jean-Claude gulped and said, "1800." Rick replied, "Thanks, see you there." as he was turning away to finish getting dressed.

Jean-Claude had to wait a little bit before he stood up so he fumbled around inside his shower kit trying to make his erection go down. Once things returned to normal, Jean-Claude entered the large shower bay filled with wet naked men.

Jean-Claude just let the hot water pour all over his body not paying any attention to the people coming and going. He was in no rush to get out of the water and the nice clean feeling he had just achieved to get back out into the dust bowl of camp. As Jean-Claude was turning around to face the full shower room he happened to look three rows directly in front of him and there, taking a shower, was a tall black man with the longest dick he ever saw. Jean-Claude took a mental picture and got out of the shower quickly as he was feeling the beginnings of an erection.

The rest of the field exercise was uneventful and, in the end, everyone survived the field exercise; barely. Jean-Claude could not get rid of this Lieutenant fast enough. "Oh well, maybe they will get rid of him while I'm on leave," Jean-Claude thought, "just 14 more days until my leave starts." Jean-Claude received another medal for his efforts in the field.

Shortly after the Battalion returned from the field the CSM was headed stateside and the new CSM had already arrived. The new CSM was CSM Benson, a tall black man that looked exactly like a teddy bear. However, when irritated he was the furthest thing from a teddy bear. The military had just put in effect a new policy there was no smoking allowed inside military buildings; Jean-Claude had forgotten and lit up a cigarette inside the office. Just as Jean-Claude was exhaling the door opened and there was CSM Benson. "What are you doing? You can't smoke inside, put that out." Jean-Claude quickly put the cigarette out and apologized. CSM just smiled and said, "Don't let it happen again." Not even a week later, Jean-Claude was the only person in the office and he couldn't leave the office so he opened the window, leaned out and lit a cigarette. A couple of puffs and there again was the CSM in the doorway. "What the hell are you doing?" CSM Benson yelled. "Hey, but technically I'm smoking outside, all be it, I'm leaning out the window to do it, but technically I'm not inside." Jean-Claude said with a smile. The CSM looked at him laughed and said, "Okay, you got me there, but none of that either, both of your feet better be outside a building touching the ground the next time I catch you smoking." "Damn" Jean-Claude thought "he just took away any loopholes."

> "Ha, leave it to you to follow instructions to the tee and find a way around them. You can be such a pill when you want to be as well you know." Ms. Wauneta said while kissing into the mirror to check her lipstick.

Leave – Back to Michigan

Jean-Claude was on his way flying back home to see his family in Michigan. He had been looking forward to this trip for a long time and was ready for just a simple quiet vacation at his parents' house doing nothing. As he boarded the plane in Frankfurt he was already starting to relax and was sleepy because Jean-Claude had begun the process of changing time zones a week ago to put himself on US time.

The plane landed at Heathrow Airport late. To be an observer of what happened next would have thought these US

Soldiers were insane. As the soldiers got off the plane, they bolted down the ramp into the corridor and at a dead run headed for the connecting flight. Solders were arriving at the gates out of breath from running to see smiling attendants who said, "Welcome to your connecting flight. We have been waiting for you to get here and after your bags are put aboard we will pull back. Enjoy your flight." Jean-Claude said, "Thank you for waiting I appreciate it." It was a huge deal to keep all these people waiting for just a handful of soldiers returning home for vacation. As the plane was pulling back the attendant came over the speaker, "Now that we have all our cargo, including soldiers returning home, we can now depart...." Jean-Claude settled into his seat and fell asleep.

Jean-Claude woke up on the flight as an attendant was walking by he asked, "How much longer ma'am?" She smiled and said, "We have about 30 minutes until we land." Jean-Claude looked out the window, the sun was rising and it was a clear day. Jean-Claude couldn't get over just how beautiful and peaceful it looked. He was finally home.

Jean-Claude got off the plane, waited to claim his duffle bag at the carousel and then off to customs. When he walked up to the counter the clerk looked up and saw the green military bag and said "Go ahead, have a nice vacation." (This was pre 9-11; you could never do that now.)

Jean-Claude saw his father waiting for him on the other side of the glass, waving he made his way through the glass maze to join his dad. Jean-Claude's dad said, "Hello, welcome home the car is this way." No hug, no handshake, "things are still the same" Jean-Claude thought and followed his dad outside. Detroit is about two and a half hours from his parent's house and the ride was a rather quiet one neither men really saying much other than small talk. Jean-Claude had gotten use to this relationship with his dad; he had always felt his dad didn't understand him. Jean-Claude was thinking, "What is going to happen when I tell

51

them I'm gay?" and the cold sweats started while his stomach churned.

Finally, they arrived home and Jean-Claude walked into the house he had spent most of his life. His little brother, Kyle, 11 and sister, Nancy, 9 ran to hug him. Jean-Claude dropped to his knees to embrace them. Nancy immediately said, "Oh, you have an earring like me, want to trade?" "Sure." Jean-Claude replied with a smile. Nancy took out one of her pink ice cream cone earrings and handed it over with her other little hand held out waiting for the diamond stud Jean-Claude was pulling out. The both put the earrings in their ears and hugged again.

Jean-Claude stood up and turned to his stepmother and said, "Hi." His step-mother sneered at him and replied, "Is there anything else we should know about you other than the earring? Go off to the Army and come back here with an earring, what are people going to think." Jean-Claude immediately got pissed and thought about saying, "well, bitch, I'm gay." He wanted to say it so bad but thought better of it and looked at the floor and said, "No." "Fine, your room is downstairs now, Kyle take him to his room." Again, no hug no nothing, "some things just never change I guess" Jean-Claude thought with a little sadness.

Jean-Claude's new room his dad built was in the basement. This was obviously the new "guestroom." Jean-Claude's old room was now Kyle's room. The room was standard, a closet, a window, a double bed, and a little writing desk. Jean-Claude tossed his duffle on the bed and lay down beside it. "This is going to be a long 30-day vacation if they are going to act like this" he thought.

It had been only ten minutes and heard his stepmother yell, "Jean-Claude come up here." Jean-Claude went up the stairs wondering what she wanted. As he came around the corner of the kitchen he saw his step-grandparents. They both rushed towards him and gave him a big hug. This made it worth the trip and Jean-Claude started to choke up because he felt loved, if only for a brief moment in time. Jean-Claude's grandpa looked at him and said, "Well now, what do we have here? Do they issue those pink ice cream cones in the Army now days?" with a sly grin and twinkle in his eye. Jean-Claude reached up to his ear, he had forgotten he still had Nancy's earring in his ear and started laughing.

Jean-Claude had requested to have a nice quiet vacation and he didn't want people in town to know he was back because he didn't want the pressure of having to go see people. However, family was different; the entire family came over for dinner that night. His other grand-parents had arrived three weeks early from Florida just so they could spend time with him. Dinner was great; it was awesome to have home cooked food again. Jean-Claude knew his stepmother, aunts and grandmas had cooked at least four days for just this one special meal. Jean-Claude's uncle Butch got the evening off to a rolling start with, "So are you seeing any girls over there?" Jean-Claude turned red and said, "No." Again, the thought of being gay came to his mind as he looked around the large table at all the faces of his family members. Jean-Claude started to think, "Oh God, I'm going to be such a disappointment to all of them."

After dinner, Jean-Claude told his dad that he needed to take a walk and would be back in a bit. Jean-Claude headed out the door happy to be away from everyone and be in a quiet space for a bit. He also wanted to have a cigarette, something he certainly was not going to let his stepmother find out about; that would just be a nasty fight. So Jean-Claude took a walk up to the farmhouse and was poking around to see what his grandpa had been up to in the shed with all the old equipment. Jean-Claude had three cigarettes before returning home, making sure he stopped off at the water trough to wash his hands and get rid of the smoke smell.

His brother and sister still had a few more days of school left and when they would head off in the morning Jean-Claude would grab a book, throw on a bathing suit and head to the pool. It had been two years since Jean-Claude had gotten a nice tan and he was determined to get one while on vacation. In the afternoon when his brother and sister got off the bus, they started pestering Jean-Claude to do things with them. Jean-Claude didn't mind, he liked being with Kyle and Nancy, they didn't judge, they just accepted people and life as it was, they were too young to have opinions yet. The three of them would play catch, ride horses, chase the cattle, go bike riding, do chores together and just be brothers and sister.

Jean-Claude kept trying to work up the courage to tell his family he was gay, but every time he would chicken out. All he could think of was how they would react, being disowned and alone in the world. However, one evening Jean-Claude thought "well today was a good quiet day, I might as well tell them now." He started out "Mom, dad, I have something to tell you. I'm falling in love with someone." His stepmother cut him off, "What do you know about love?" Jean-Claude was instantly angry, "what?" Again, his stepmother said, "What do you know about love?" Jean-Claude fired back, "How the fuck would anyone know growing up in this house?" and he turned and went down into the basement.

Jean-Claude was pacing back and forth in the room muttering, "What the hell? Again, with the controlling bullshit, why can't I just be me? What is her fucking issue?" Jean-Claude went upstairs and out the back door unnoticed to get away and smoke. As Jean-Claude was walking down the road heading towards the forest he started to cry. He knew what was going to happen if he told them he was gay; he would be shut out and have no family. A wave of sadness and despair came over him and he just fell down sobbing. He knew life would never be the same again; he was starting a new journey alone.

Jean-Claude became very angry and pulled back from his family. He didn't want to get hurt when the time came to tell his family about being gay. He turned off his emotions and began acting like nothing could hurt him. This was his way of coping with the disappointments in life.

Jean-Claude's stepmother approached and said, "Since you are not going to be here for your birthday, Kyle and Nancy want to give you a party." Jean-Claude smiled and said, "Okay." While thinking, "Such innocence, I hope they will be okay when I'm gone."

The night before he was to leave for Germany the entire family got together to celebrate his birthday. It was a nice party and Jean-Claude tried to take in as many memories as he could because he knew sometime in the near future he would have to tell his family he was gay. He just could not go on feeling like he was hiding from everyone and lying all the time. It was eating at him. He tried to enjoy the party but his mind kept getting pulled back into his inner thoughts.

The next day Jean-Claude's dad drove him the two and a half hours back to Detroit to catch the flight to Germany. His dad pulled up to the front doors of the airport and said, "Here we are, good luck and we will see you later." Jean-Claude pulled his duffle bag out of the backseat and with a nod of his head to his dad he turned and walked into the airport. Jean-Claude started to choke up with the thought of being alone again. As he checked in for his flight, Jean-Claude struggled to keep it together. He knew soon enough his world would come crashing down around him when he finally got the courage to tell his family he was gay.

"Oh Chickie, we all go through a painful process of coming out. It is very different for each person and it cannot be rushed in any manner. If a person is not ready, they are not ready. You just were not ready to tell them yet." Ms. Wauneta explained gently while applying her mascara.

The flight back to Germany was a nice flight because there were not many people on the flight so everyone could spread out and lie across the seats and go to sleep. Jean-Claude woke up a few hours into the flight and the cabin had the low lights on and a flight attendant had placed a blanket over him and sat a pillow at his feet.

Jean-Claude arrived at Frankfurt airport at 2300 and made a phone call to the Duty Officer to send the van for him. Since he had some time to kill, Jean-Claude sat down, had dinner and read a newspaper. At the appointed time, Jean-Claude walked out the front door and around the corner was the familiar green VW bus to pick him up. "Hey Sergeant," Jean-Claude greeted the sergeant. The sergeant grunted and said, "You have to report to the CSM when we get back to Battalion. "Odd, why did they send a sergeant to pick him up and why does he have to see the CSM this late at night? Maybe they moved up a field exercise again." Jean-Claude thought quietly to himself.

When Jean-Claude exited the van at Battalion Headquarters the duty officer was standing at the door and said, "Follow me, leave your bags someone will get them for you." Jean-Claude dropped his bag and simply followed the officer up the stairs; it was now almost 0200. Jean-Claude entered the CSM's office and made his report and the CSM looked up and said, "Sit." "Okay this is strange" Jean-Claude was thinking, "CSM never has anyone sit in his office." CSM closed the file he was working on and speaking as if it was a father to a son said, "There was an accident while you were gone and it affects you directly." Pausing to look at Jean-Claude and make sure he was registering his words, CSM continued, "Specialist Small has died. He was running and his heart exploded. A German doctor was driving by when it happened and tried everything to save Small to no use." Jean-Claude was in shock because he and Small would go running together often and he was so young; only 20 years old. CSM continued, "You sleep in the 26th Support Battalion building tonight and more permanent housing will be handled tomorrow. Go see your CQ he will take you to your room." Jean-Claude walked over to HHQ in a daze, not feeling anything; the CQ stopped him at the front door and said, "This way." Jean-Claude simply followed as he was led up to the third floor of the Support building. Jean-Claude was put in a four-person room by himself. (This would turn out to be his permanent AO during his assignment in Germany.)

Jean-Claude showed up for morning formation ready to take part in PT, but the First Sergeant stopped him and said, "Go back to bed and meet in my office at 0900." "Okay" Jean-Claude replied as he turned back around. Promptly at 0900 Jean-Claude met with the First Sergeant in his office. The First Sergeant quietly said, "So you have been brought up-to-date I understand. You will move all your stuff out of your room after this meeting into the room where you spent the night last night. You will report for the 0800 formation tomorrow." With that Jean-Claude headed upstairs to start moving out of his old room that he had shared with Small.

When Jean-Claude entered the room, it was empty except for his locker. It felt strange to be in such an empty room. The move didn't take too long since most of Jean-Claude's civilian clothes were still packed in his duffle bag. Jean-Claude ran into Mason from his shop and Mason asked, "Do you need help?" "No, I got it thanks." Jean-Claude replied; no other words were exchanged.

Small's death had an impact on the S-4 shop; everyone kept quiet and went about their business in a daze. On Friday, everyone in HHQ Company showed up for the 0800 formation in their Class A uniforms. The entire Company was attending a memorial service for Small that morning. Jean-Claude sat listening to some of the nice words from fellow soldiers and tried to hold back the tears. As Jean-Claude turned to check on the members of his shop, they all had tears streaming down their faces. Standing at attention, for the first time, Jean-Claude heard the lone call of a bugle playing Taps. Jean-Claude could never listen to Taps being played again and not think of the deaths of fellow soldiers.

Griggs, the Battalion Legal Clerk, was assigned the horrible task of accompanying Small back to his family. Everyone else was to start preparing for deployment to another field exercise.

Jean-Claude was on the warpath after Small's death, it was as if he didn't go on vacation and the stress levels were right back to the same level as before he left for the States. Jean-Claude forgot about himself, how he felt and buried himself in work. This was a safe and secure place where he didn't need to deal with feelings, just make things happen. Jean-Claude was chewing up his assigned soldiers for anything and everything in site that they did wrong. It was a stressful time for everyone.

Jean-Claude started looking for someone to step into his shoes and take a leadership role. Jean-Claude decided he would put Mason in charge of the advanced party to see how he would handle the pressure. Jean-Claude gave Mason the assignment saying, "this is all yours, if you have any questions, just ask and we will help. But you need to plan and carry out the entire Advance Party until we arrive five days after you." Mason did an exceptional job and would receive a medal for his efforts.

This field exercise was an easy one for Jean-Claude because he now had the experience needed to make things go smoothly and it was a fairly small exercise without many large movements. Jean-Claude got bored sitting at camp and decided to send one of the company supply sergeants to the rear to pick up the mail and take care of business. He would be gone for three days so Jean-Claude stepped into the company take his place. It was fun for Jean-Claude to be at a company again, less to worry about and more contact with the soldiers in the field.

When Jean-Claude returned to camp three days later, he had to deal with the things that were placed on hold while he was out in the field. It was late in the evening when he finally got to take a shower. This shower was merely five showerheads lined up against a wall in an L-shape. When Jean-Claude entered the shower it was empty as he turned on the water he heard the door opening. Turning around he saw the new lieutenant that had been assigned to Charlie Company. He had blond hair, blue eyes and was built from working out. Jean-Claude quickly turned and faced the wall to start taking a long hot shower. He turned around and stole a look at the lieutenant, "wow, he is hot" is all Jean-Claude could think of at the time. The lieutenant took a very quick shower and headed out. Jean-Claude was alone with his thoughts of the lieutenant which were interrupted by the door opening again. Jean-Claude turned and looked and it was a very short medic from HHQ. Jean-Claude turned back around as he only knew this medic in passing.

Visions of the lieutenant kept entering Jean-Claude's head and he was starting to grow erect; so he turned to the corner of the shower to hide it from the medic. Suddenly the medic had grabbed Jean-Claude's cock and there was no stopping the erection now. Jean-Claude took a look at the short medic and thought, "God certainly has a sense of humor. The lieutenant was this mass of a man with a tiny dick and this short dude has a huge dick." The medic got on his knees and started sucking on Jean-Claude. Jean-Claude was extremely nervous and told the medic, "Stop before someone comes in and we get caught." The medic grinned and said, "Let's get out of here and go to my APC in the motor pool."

Jean-Claude dropped his stuff off on his bunk and told the guys he was going out for a walk. He saw the medic slowly walking towards the motor pool glancing back every now and again to see if Jean-Claude was following. Once the medic knew Jean-Claude was following he picked up the pace towards the APC. When they arrived the medic unlocked the back troop door and they jumped inside. They started feeling each other and having oral sex when all the sudden the medic said, "I want to fuck you." Jean-Claude looked at the medic like he was crazy, "what do you mean, not with that huge thing you are not, besides I've never done that and not sure I want to try with that big thing." The medic looked disappointed, but understood, and they stuck with oral sex.

"Oh my, a shower scene and a motor pool scene! Well you didn't lack in the adventure area of sexual encounters did you now? I feel the vapors coming again." Ms. Wauneta grinned with a twinkle in her eye as she was brushing one of her wigs.

Returning from the field, Jean-Claude set to work preparing for his departure to PLDC. Ensuring everyone would be able to cover his job while he was away, since they would not be able to speak with him directly while he was in school. Additionally, he had to complete Mason's paperwork to get a medal approved for his efforts in the field. Jean-Claude spent nearly the entire two weeks writing the report and recommendation for Mason's medal with the help of Captain Ryan.

It was time for him to leave to Primary Leadership Development School (PLDC) for 30 days. While he was attending PLDC the First Sergeant was getting a replacement for the captain's driver as the old driver was rotating back stateside. The school was up in northern Germany in the middle of a forest. The weather sucked; every day was cold, wet, rainy and above all else muddy. The mud was the worst because uniforms had to be pressed and shined every night for the next day. Mud is just one of the elements that can destroy a shine on a boot and getting the shine back takes work. The guys in Jean-Claude's platoon got together and they rotated boot duty among themselves so people could get some sleep; two hours on shining all the boots and off to sleep. This was a neat trick as the instructors were getting frustrated with Jean-Claude's platoon since they could not issue demerits like the other platoons.

Finally the last week of PLDC; an old fashion "lives in your little tiny pup tent with another guy" field exercise. On the second day Jean-Claude said to no one in particular, "This sucks, I'm cold, wet and muddy with no way to get dry." Everyone agreed and they all just kept pushing on knowing it would soon be over.

The final day of PLDC arrived and graduation was held in the center of camp standing in about three inches of water and muck. After graduation everyone broke apart to find their rides back to their units. Jean-Claude wandered about for a little when he saw his Battalion's little green van. Jean-Claude tossed his gear in the back and climbed in the front seat and said, "Hi, I'm ready to get the hell out of here and dry off." They headed out for the three hour trip back home.

Sam

After completion of PLDC all Jean-Claude could think of was getting his gear cleaned up, taking a shower and repacking everything for the upcoming field exercise. Jean-Claude arrived back at HHQ Friday evening. While checking in with the HHQ Staff Duty Officer and was advised that a new driver was assigned to S-4. "Fuck, I have to deal with this kid because we are going back into the field Monday morning." So Jean-Claude went up to his room, dropped off his pack and took a quick shower and headed over to Echo Company to meet Sam. Jean-Claude checked in with the CQ who advised him of Sam's room and said, "Just go down there, he is in there, he never leaves." "Hmm, maybe a good sign if he is not getting out much, he would be available at times" Jean-Claude was thinking as he walked down the hall.

Knocking on the door got a yell, "Come in." Jean-Claude entered the room and introduced himself and Sam stood up and said, "I'm the new driver." Jean-Claude was in no mood to be trifled with and could have cared less what anyone thought of him. He was already thinking of all the stuff that would need to be done before the field problem; having to deal with a newly assigned driver was not at the top of his list of things to accomplish. Jean-Claude took a seat on the back of the couch with his feet in the couch with Sam sitting in the chair directly in front of him they started to have a conversation. Jean-Claude was looking at Sam while he was talking with him and was thinking to himself, "Oh shit, this guy is gorgeous!" Jean-Claude being afraid of being found out that he was having any thoughts like this began going hard core military.

Sam was taller than Jean-Claude. He had light blond hair, piercing blue eyes that could see through you and a chest that all you could think about was laying your head on. Sam weighed roughly 180 pounds, with arms that all Jean-Claude wanted to do was melt into them. It was obvious to Jean-Claude that Sam lifted weights regularly. Jean-Claude could not let Sam know he had made such an assessment and quickly took control of the conversation. Sam made this easy for Jean-Claude as Jean-Claude was his superior and his new boss. This should have been Sam's first inkling that Jean-Claude could be a real prick. Jean-Claude turned into a monster if he thought anyone was close to finding out how he felt inside. This, without exception, was one of those times and a full frontal assault was engaged to keep Sam from thinking Jean-Claude was gay.

As Jean-Claude headed back to his room to do laundry and knowing Sam would be working closely with him, he kept thinking about how hot Sam was. Jean-Claude kept thinking, "This is going to be a problem." "How the hell am I going to deal with this, I'm always going to have to cover up how I feel." were the only thoughts going through Jean-Claude's mind. After laundry was completed and lying in piles around the room to be packed up the next day for deployment, Jean-Claude went to sleep. Waking the next morning, Jean-Claude ran to the mess hall for breakfast and back to begin packing for Monday, Sam was at the forefront of his mind and constantly nagging at his thoughts.

> "Hmm, Ms. Wauneta smells a big mess coming with this guy Sam. I can tell by the way you look while talking about him. I've seen that look before on myself when I think of my first love." Ms. Wauneta explained while placing a box of tissues near Jean-Claude.

Sam remained with his company until the official transfer to HHQ was approved and Sam would be moving into Jean-Claude's room as there were no other rooms available. This was unusual because Jean-Claude was a Corporal and Sam was a PFC, enlisted and NCOs never shared quarters.

Jean-Claude and Sam shared a four-person room, just the two of them. Saturday night Sam and Jean-Claude were talking about a bunch of stuff; however, soon the conversation turned to a dangerous place for Jean-Claude. Sam kept saying, "Birds of a feather flock together." Jean-Claude looked at him like he just fell from another planet. Jean-Claude had no idea what he was talking about and after about 45 minutes of going round and around babbling like two fools, Jean-Claude reached over and touched Sam's leg. The talking finally stopped as it sunk in that each were trying to come out to each other without saying, "I'm gay."

Jean-Claude just looked at Sam, scared out of his mind not sure what was going to happen next. He was so scared Sam would use this new information to turn him in and he would get kicked out of the military as a fag. Then Sam came close and kissed Jean-Claude. That was all Jean-Claude needed to let loose the pent up feelings and frustrations in his mind and just went forward without thinking. Soon, Jean-Claude was taking off Sam's shirt and revealing his smooth built chest, peeling off his pants and underwear, feeling Sam's body next to him, Jean-Claude was in a blissful state. For the moment, Jean-Claude wasn't thinking, he was just letting the moment take him where it may. Sam was peeling off Jean-Claude's clothes as fast as he could as well. As they were kissing, feeling their bodies against each other Jean-Claude was in heaven.

As things heated up and Jean-Claude quickly went down on Sam, hearing his moans of pleasure gave Jean-Claude a feeling of happiness and self worth in having Sam enjoy what was happening. Then Sam went down on Jean-Claude. Jean-Claude almost jumped out of his skin, this had never happened before where someone was sucking on his cock because they liked him. Before it just felt like someone returning a favor. Jean-Claude was overcome with emotions and turned them off and refused to think about anything other than enjoying the moment with Sam.

When they were finished having sex, Jean-Claude sent Sam back to his AO in the front of the room. Jean-Claude thought it would be illogical for Sam to stay in bed with him; it simply never occurred to him that Sam might want to stay and sleep next to him. Jean-Claude started feeling guilty, dirty, hateful and inadequate as a person. Jean-Claude kept thinking, "What am I going to do now?" "What if this gets out?" "What if we had gotten caught?" "How am I going to face him in the morning?" "What is going to happen when I see him tomorrow?" "What if someone sees through either one of us and discovers our secret?" "Everything I've worked so hard for will all be gone if anyone finds out." "Shit, this is really bad, not only am I having sex with a guy, but he is my direct report, they don't let straight guys get away with that, I'm in so much trouble." "I have to control this somehow." Jean-Claude started to think of his parents and he started playing the conversation in his head from his stepmother saying stuff like "You make me sick," "You can't even be with a woman." "You are not my son." "How can you embarrass the family like this?" "You disgust me." To the thoughts of his father sitting there looking in complete shock at him. All the while this shrill woman just kept making her point

64

that Jean-Claude was nothing and would never amount to anything that they could ever be proud.

"Oh Chickie, you had no idea how to cope with all this stuff going on did you? There was no one you could talk to about this stuff? That is something I don't understand about the Don't Ask, Don't Tell policy, how are these guys supposed to figure out their lives if they can't tell anyone?" Ms. Wauneta stomped her foot for emphasis as she spoke.

A very complicated relationship developed between Sam and Jean-Claude. Jean-Claude made it complicated; Sam, on the other hand, knew exactly what he wanted. Jean-Claude had no clue how to be in a relationship, how to be honest with himself, express his true feelings with another human being, or how to let someone love him. Jean-Claude engaged the only thing he knew, as he would open up, his fears would take over and he would close down again.

The next day came at 0430 to get ready for PT formation at 0500. Sam and Jean-Claude got up and Sam said, "Good morning." Jean-Claude just grunted and kept getting dressed; he could not get out of the room fast enough. Jean-Claude did PT all the time half paying attention to what was being called out. The exercises were drilled into his head and he barely listened anyway most of the time at PT. Jean-Claude just kept playing the recording of his stepmother's shrill voice in his head rebuking him over and over for what he had done with Sam.

Relief came over Jean-Claude when Sam ran off to the mess hall for breakfast instead of hitting the showers like Jean-Claude right after PT. Jean-Claude said to himself, "thank God I don't have to see him in the shower because I don't know what would happen." Jean-Claude took a shower and got ready and went to the office to avoid being in the room when Sam returned from the mess hall.

At 0800 work formation, Jean-Claude didn't go because he was getting ready to leave for the field and was getting everything ready for when the S-4 guys came into the office. All the sudden the door opened and the guys were coming into work, time had escaped Jean-Claude and he was now running late. Then he noticed Sam was not with the group that came into the office. "Hmm, I wonder where he is," Jean-Claude thought, he didn't want to ask the guys where he was because he was afraid someone would figure it out. Assignments were handed out to everyone and off they went to prepare to go out to the field. Some of the guys were leaving today and others would be following two days later. The door the office opened up again and it was the S-4 officer following up on the assignments and plans for the deployment. "Fuck, this is not good, now I'm really going to be late getting my stuff loaded and we have to go soon." Jean-Claude said as he just went through the motions of filling in the S-4 officer.

Finally, Jean-Claude advised the S-4 officer he had to go get his stuff and get ready to go. Jean-Claude was running out the door, down the stairs and up the hill to the billets when at the top of the hill he saw Sam standing there with a bunch of stuff packed in the Humvee. Jean-Claude said, "Give me a few and I'll get my bags and get them down here, we shouldn't be late." Sam just looked at Jean-Claude with a grin and said, "Your bags are already packed in the Humvee." Jean-Claude came to a dead stop and said, "Okay, well then let's get going and figure out our spot in the convoy."

It was unusual for Jean-Claude to be riding in the Humvee with Sam as Sam was the S-4 officer's driver. Jean-Claude had switched into full military mode and while all the preparations were being made to leave never gave Sam a second thought until now…"why did he put my stuff in the truck? I never asked him to do that, what is he trying to pull?" Sam was bouncing around like someone had lit matches between his toes and smiling his cute smile. Jean-Claude was oblivious to why and just thought this was how Sam acted since they had just met. Jean-Claude didn't understand that Sam did this because he cared for him.

> "Oh how cute, the boy was very smitten with you! Let me guess you never figured that out did you? Sometimes you can be very hardheaded. We have to write things on a 2x4 and smack you over the head to get things to sink in to that thick skull of yours." Ms. Wauneta said while looking disapprovingly at Jean-Claude.

The entire field problem went off without a hitch and Jean-Claude and Sam really didn't see much of each other because they had different assignments. For Jean-Claude this was just fine since he had to work to keep things running. Now that he was a Corporal he had more responsibilities and would be held to a higher standard as an NCO. If there was anything about Jean-Claude doing the best that he could do in the military was not enough he had to be perfect. He thought this would keep anyone from guessing his big secret that he was gay. Jean-Claude was a by the book NCO, something that can make enemies quickly especially being in supply where you can become the lynchpin in someone succeeding their goals and assignments.

Returning to garrison, Jean-Claude was relieved to be back in garrison where schedules would settle down and life would go on in a normal way. Well, what is considered normal for a military lifestyle. But that was not what was planned for Jean-Claude as he quickly found out. The very night after returned from the field Sam wanted to have sex again. This was something that was out of the question for Jean-Claude at the time. There was no real reason just that Jean-Claude didn't want to have sex. Jean-Claude pushed back hard on Sam and made him go back to his AO very unceremoniously. Sam's feelings were the least of Jean-Claude's worries. Jean-Claude laid in bed trying to figure out why Sam wanted to have sex with him. This certainly was not his experience with other guys and why would Sam want to be with him anyway. Jean-Claude finally just stopped thinking about it and went to sleep.

It was nice to be back, after the clean up from returning, putting everything away and settling back into garrison life it allowed everyone a little more time to do what they wanted. One thing that Jean-Claude missed while being in the field was his long runs by himself; it was the only time he was ever by himself physically; mentally was a different story. Mentally Jean-Claude could tune out the world around him in a busy airport and not realize there were other people around.

On this particular evening as Jean-Claude was getting ready to go off on his run, Sam came in the room and asked, "Do you want to go to the gym and lift some weights?" Jean-Claude thought, "What the hell is this guy asking me that for, do I look like I lift weights? The weights will crush my small body!" but instead said, "No, I'm going running." And out the door Jean-Claude headed, not looking back or sticking around to find out if Sam wanted to join. Jean-Claude wanted and needed to be by himself, he needed to sort this mess he had gotten himself into.

As Jean-Claude set out running, he let his mind wander and allow the thoughts and feelings come as they may. This was the only time that Jean-Claude allowed his mind to be completely honest with himself or anyone for that matter. The first thing that came to his mind was how friggin' hot Sam was, "My God, how gorgeous is he?" A sly smile came across his face because Jean-Claude knew he had slept with one of the hottest guys on base. This happiness was quickly squashed with the thought of his family. The guilt started pouring in and as tears were streaming down his face Jean-Claude began the process of trying to deal with disappointing his family.

"Why do I like Sam?" Jean-Claude thought; he didn't know the answer any more than "Fuck, he is hot." Jean-Claude couldn't figure out his attraction to Sam, he just knew he liked him a lot. "How the hell are you going to handle seeing him every day and not get caught and kicked out?" Jean-Claude didn't have an answer to that either. Then suddenly it hit Jean-Claude: "Don't tell anyone, don't let anyone know, hide your feelings, don't you dare let anyone into your feelings, you don't know what he will do with your feelings, shut it down now and keep 'in control' as much as possible." "Okay, I'm 'in control' – control is the key, control the information and control your feelings," there Jean-Claude thought, the decision is made, I can move on now.

Jean-Claude stopped running and looked around, he was in the middle of the forest not far from the Kaserne. As he slowly figured out he was on the far back side of the forest, he had run much further than he had thought. This would occur over and over where he would start running and not remember where or how he got someplace, later in life, it would occur while driving, a complete blank. Jean-Claude turned and started heading back home.

When Jean-Claude got home he hopped into the shower and began settling in for the night and then it happened. Sam started talking and the next thing Jean-Claude and Sam were wrapped in each other's arms. The simple acts of Sam putting his arms around Jean-Claude made him feel safe and secure, a feeling that Jean-Claude never before experienced. Again, after sex Jean-Claude sent Sam back to his own AO and the cycle repeated itself, the shame, guilt and thoughts began all over again. All the questions that Jean-Claude thought he had resolved came rushing back; it wasn't enough to be "in control." Again, Jean-Claude fell asleep crying softly so Sam would not hear.

As the months went on, Sam and Jean-Claude became closer and closer, to the point Jean-Claude was consumed by Sam. Jean-Claude thought "How the hell did Sam get so much control? I cannot allow this, I will just get hurt and he can never know about the things that happened to me in the past." Then there came a point where Sam told Jean-Claude a story of a much older male and he; which would be considered rape of an underage individual. Jean-Claude didn't know what to say, the feelings of his own molestation came flooding back all at once. Jean-Claude simply snapped those emotions back into their box and dealt with Sam by pushing him away again. Sam would always come forward and Jean-Claude would always push back. This cycle continued for several months.

One morning, Jean-Claude pulled PT duty; since he was a junior NCO this was one of the required tasks, among other things. So the exercises went off pretty much okay, as they were assigned by the First Sergeant and there was little to no leeway as to what the exercises were going to be for the morning. Then it came time for the Company to head out for the run. Imagine a Company roughly 1,300 strong all marching and running in step, you would think it was pretty easy, but it has its own challenges. Jean-Claude had led platoon size formations all of his military career, this was the first time he had the entire company to command and one this size was a daunting challenge. As Jean-Claude was preparing the Company to go running, Sam jumped out and got his vest for 'road guard' duty. Jean-Claude caught him out of the corner of his eye and wondered, "What is he doing, he is not a runner" because he had never seen Sam in this role before.

It was a disaster to say the least; Jean-Claude could not keep the entire Company in step. The formation looked like a caterpillar with several bad legs and it was limping along. Jean-Claude finally gave up and had one of the senior NCOs take control. Within four calls the senior NCO had the entire company on the same foot. Jean-Claude thought, "This isn't so bad, now I can just run with the company and not worry too much about the formation."

As luck would have it the Commander decided that he was going to take the Company up a notorious hill on the back of the Kaserne. This hill is known for getting guys to drop out of formation because they are tired and are not runners. Jean-Claude was a runner by nature, so the hill was nothing for him since he ran this hill every evening after work. However, Jean-Claude was running backwards, up the hill checking on the formation and how many people were dropping out of formation when he saw Sam waived his arms as he said, "Look out." Too late, Jean-Claude fell over backwards over the branch that was lying in the middle of the road. Down he went, rolled over and back up again facing the back of the formation and just kept running. Jean-Claude was turning red as Sam ran up and was laughing, "Are you okay?" "Yes, I'm fine" Jean-Claude replied. Sam kept laughing as he ran off ahead. "Bastard" Jean-Claude mumbled under his breath.

When they returned to the barracks, Jean-Claude had Sam take a look and see how much damage was caused. Jean-Claude had a nice road rash from the top of his butt up the spine to the shoulder blades. It was bleeding a little and Sam gently cleaned it off. Jean-Claude was so embarrassed and Sam was still laughing saying, "I will never get that image out of my head, you falling ass over tea kettle…" laughing harder and unable to finish the sentence. Jean-Claude had to admit it was funny too looking back.

> "HA-HA! Funny, I can imagine you rolling over…awww what a blow to your little ego too. I know you and how embarrassed you get when attention is on you. Sam must have loved it because you were finally human to him."
> Ms. Wauneta laughed as she stood up to look at the rack of clothes.

Then it happened, Sam said, "I love you." Without thinking Jean-Claude said, "I love you too." With those words a new level of the relationship had opened. Sam had managed to break his way past all the walls of protection Jean-Claude had erected.

The sex between Sam and Jean-Claude was frequent. Imagine two 19-year olds living together in a quasi-relationship and free time together. Sam began teaching Jean-Claude the joys of anal sex and letting yourself go with another person. Jean-Claude was experiencing things he never thought possible with another person. Sam opened a whole entire new avenue of life for Jean-Claude. Jean-Claude was falling madly in love with Sam; he was beginning to lose himself in Sam's arms and love. Sam's love was so pure and harsh that Jean-Claude did not understand just how much love he was being given by Sam.

As time progressed, Jean-Claude would get a little brave at times and show he was vulnerable by saying to Sam, "143" in the office. This was Sam's and Jean-Claude's way of saying "I love you" without anyone figuring out what they were talking about. To Jean-Claude just saying he loved Sam was a huge risk. Jean-Claude was afraid of getting hurt and by saying that you love someone or something only meant it would be taken away by someone or something; just because. It could be used against you in any number of imaginable ways.

Even though Sam and Jean-Claude had said they loved each other, there was never a discussion about the relationship; it seemed to have just been assumed by each other. Jean-Claude didn't need this to outlined to him, but he did. He needed Sam to say look, we are in a relationship and only you and I will be in this relationship. Jean-Claude could not be left to his own devices since he had no clue about being in a relationship, let alone having someone love him. Jean-Claude had no concept of how to handle, let alone deal, with someone who loved him just for him. Jean-Claude had firmly entrenched in his mind that if someone said, "I love you" that meant they wanted something more than Jean-Claude could give. He would just be disappointed in the end anyway…nothing this good could last.

This feeling made Jean-Claude think of the Annie Lennox song "Everyone Wants Something," the words are perfect for how Jean-Claude was feeling.

Sam and Jean-Claude had decided to get off the Kaserne and have dinner at Burger King down the street. While they were sitting eating dinner, Jean-Claude noticed a table full of gay men across the dining area. Jean-Claude made degrading comments about the group since he knew they were gay from the "underground." Jean-Claude didn't want to be associated with them for fear of being labeled gay for just hanging out with them. Sam was completely unfazed by other gay men around; he was so confident with whom he was it just didn't matter. Jean-Claude was a bit jealous of this confidence, but then again, "Sam was built like a brick shithouse, who in their right mind would ever accuse him of being gay?" Jean-Claude thought.

Jean-Claude took Sam to Frankfurt with him one weekend. Previously Jean-Claude would go by himself and give evasive answers when asked about where he went because he didn't want anyone to know where he was going. He was taking Sam to the location he had found with the help of the prostitute giving him the business card. Going to Frankfurt was like going to another country for Jean-Claude. No one knew him, he could be a little more of himself and hide among the many people in Frankfurt just going about their business of living. Jean-Claude and Sam hopped on the train from Aschaffenburg to Frankfurt which was about a 40-minute ride, take a walk for about 20 minutes and they arrived at a club called Lucky Manhattan.

Lucky Manhattans appeared to be an old theater converted into a bar. It still had all the overhead lights and the sign above the bar was a huge multicolored light bulb sign pointing the way into the front door. This bar was a drag bar and frequented on Fridays and Saturdays by soldiers from all over Germany. This is where the soldiers would meet with friends before going out to party at a local club for the night. If one wanted to spend the night in Frankfurt there was a hotel nearby that was cheap where you could get a 'crash pad' for the night. If the hotel was not your style one could go a couple of blocks away and there was a very active bath house where one could hang out until the trains started running in the morning. Jean-Claude had done this in the past.

"Well I be damned; you have been a lover of drag queens way back then Chickie! Who would have thought?" Ms. Wauneta smiled.

Sam looked like a kid at Christmas when he entered Lucky Manhattan. Jean-Claude smiled and just looked at Sam having a good time, Jean-Claude started feeling good about bringing Sam and showing him where he was going; finally Jean-Claude wouldn't have to hide from Sam. After a couple of drinks, meeting a couple of guys they headed out the door. Sam asked, "Where are we going?" Jean-Claude replied, "Just around the corner to a club.", they walked out one door, down the street a half block and around the corner. Immediately they turned into a nondescript doorway made of metal and they were at C4. Jean-Claude didn't know if this was even the name of the club, but he didn't care. This club was huge and filled with men from all over Germany, both Germans and US soldiers. All seemed not have a care in the world when they were at C4; it was as if going to a place where there were only gay people and straight people were the minority.

As you enter C4 through the huge metal doors all you can see are the stairs leading down into the club with a bouncer at the bottom checking IDs. Once past the bouncer, as you look into the club is a huge bar with a few people sitting at the stools. When they went either right or left through a doorway you would enter the main area of the club. Along the left wall were banquettes for sitting and chatting with old or new friends you might have just met that night. There is another bar found against the wall where the doors are located and in the middle is the dance floor. It is easy to disappear from someone inside and just observe. This latter was Jean-Claude's favorite part, he could just watch people and their interactions.

It didn't take Jean-Claude long to figure out that this might not have been a good idea, as all attention seemed to turn to Sam. Well, what had Jean-Claude expected with the way Sam looked, he was an Adonis to gay men. As Sam was out meeting people, he kept looking at Jean-Claude as if to say, come on join us, have fun, relax; but this was the furthest thing from Jean-Claude's mind. Jean-Claude was feeling, for the first time, jealously. Jean-Claude began the downward spiral riding the big green monster of jealousy. As anyone knows this is never a good ride, nor does it ever have a good ending for any of the parties involved.

Again the monster within Jean-Claude broke out like the possessiveness of an impetuous child with a new toy. All Jean-Claude could think was, "Mine, mine, go away, stop talking." Things reached a point that Jean-Claude demanded that they leave and Sam obliged, reluctantly. The ride home was a quiet one between Sam and Jean-Claude. When they arrived at home each went to their own beds. The cycle started all again...Jean-Claude was pushing Sam away. Jean-Claude had been hurt at C4 and he went to bed feeling hurt and betrayed. None of Sam's actions in any way should have hurt Jean-Claude. However, Jean-Claude was not use to a relationship and love was an idea he did not fully understand, nor appreciate and Sam was bearing the brunt of the abuse handed out by Jean-Claude.

> "Oh good God, Jean-Claude, you were in love with the guy! What did you expect to happen when he was getting the attention? Did you think it would just all be okay? I know you don't get jealous now Jean-Claude, but it happens to everyone at some point." Ms. Wauneta was

poking her finger in the air at Jean-Claude as she was talking.

On another excursion to Frankfurt, Sam and Jean-Claude met a guy and decided to take him back to the barracks for the night. Since they had the room to themselves and there was no CQ to sneak past so this was not a problem. This was to be Jean-Claude's first three-way. Everything started out well enough until Jean-Claude started to get jealous. He did not like someone else with Sam sexually and pulled away. Sam knew there was a problem, but could not express it. The next day Sam looked at Jean-Claude and said, "Well that was not how it was suppose to go, everyone should be more involved. Jean-Claude just said "Oh." Jean-Claude made the decision to make sure that never happened again.

Todde passed and soon it was New Years Eve; time to party! Jean-Claude and Sam planned on going up to Frankfurt to C4 and meet up with some friends that Sam had made. Off to Lucky Manhattans then over to C4 they went. The party theme at C4 was "Miss Piggy" complete with pink pigs hanging by their tails on streamers from the ceiling, a Miss Piggy champagne bar and confetti at least a good two inches thick. Sam and Jean-Claude were having a good time dancing and just being free among all the gay men partying. Sam seemed to be having time of his life dancing with the guys and just generally having fun. Jean-Claude was happy for Sam; it was so nice seeing him like this. Jean-Claude was feeling loved, cared about, and safe; he was starting to settle down with his emotions towards Sam.

"Ha, Miss Piggy, what a great idea for a party! Sounds like it was a blast Chickie." Ms. Wauneta stated excitedly.

After partying into the wee hours of the morning, Sam and Jean-Claude were leaving. They essentially closed down the place. To get out of C4 they walked toward the stairs heading out the main door, past a bouncer at the bottom of the stairs. The bouncer looked at Sam who was walking ahead of Jean-Claude and the bouncer said, "Well we know who the bottom is in this relationship." Without missing a beat and glancing back at Jean-Claude with a smirk Sam said, "Don't assume anything." Jean-Claude and Sam looked at each other and laughed as they walked up the stairs.

Exiting the door the cold January air hit them; Jean-Claude started closing up again, he was back in the real world where everyone was "straight." Sam saw the look on Jean-Claude's face and grimaced at Jean-Claude; this was the first time Jean-Claude had noticed this look and took note of it quickly and remained quiet. When they arrived home Sam and Jean-Claude were so tired they fell asleep in Jean-Claude's bed.

Jean-Claude woke up the next morning next to Sam who was already awake and staring at him. Jean-Claude smiled, kissed Sam and snuggled closer and closed his eyes taking a deep breath drawing Sam's scent into him. At that moment it was if the entire world had stopped and everything was okay. It didn't matter if he liked Sam, it didn't matter what anyone thought, it didn't matter what the Army said, all that mattered was he was safe in Sam's arms. All the bad things that could happen or that had happened couldn't get to Jean-Claude; just as long as he stayed put in Sam's arms. Jean-Claude would later learn that he would never quite get this feeling ever again with another person. However, at this stage Jean-Claude couldn't see his hand in front of his face with a flashlight as he was so ill equipped to deal with these emotions.

Finally, Jean-Claude really woke up and Sam wouldn't let him out of bed. Jean-Claude just gave up trying to get out of bed and just kissed Sam passionately and they made love. There was no hurry to get out of bed. The thought of food didn't cross their minds; Jean-Claude was content to just lie safely in Sam's arms and for the first time, didn't think about anything other than how much he loved Sam. This was short lived.

Jean-Claude got out of bed and wandered across the hall to take a shower. He was the only one in the shower. Sam and he never took a shower together for fear their cocks would give them away by getting hard in the shower where anyone could walk in on them.

Jean-Claude finally got some hot water, "crappy-ass boilers" he thought "water had to travel up the basement four floors up and it took forever." Jean-Claude got under the showers and started thinking about Sam, the night they had together and this morning. Jean-Claude started crying and trying to get air, he had never cried so hard in his life. "Why does Sam love me?" "What does he see in me?" "Can I love him the same back?" "Sam shouldn't be with me, it will not end well." "I'm just going to get hurt." Jean-Claude couldn't help the feelings that were overwhelming him. When he went back into the room, he looked at the floor so Sam could not see he had been crying and start asking questions.

> "Honey, you still do the same thing to this day. You question everything to death and end up thinking you are not good enough for anyone so you undermine the relationship so you don't get hurt. I've seen you do this several times over the years." Ms. Wauneta looked directly at Jean-Claude while delivering the lecture.

When Sam was getting ready to go into the shower, Jean-Claude looked down at the floor and saw all the confetti strewn all over the place. Jean-Claude looked at Sam, pointed and just started to laugh. They would be finding this confetti for months afterwards as it seems to have gotten into everything possible.

As Sam was in the shower, Jean-Claude reached a point and decided: he was going to accept that he was gay. Finally, Jean-Claude made the turn and started to deal with the emotions of admitting to himself that he was gay. Jean-Claude never discussed this with Sam because he thought Sam would just laugh and call him stupid. Jean-Claude still didn't trust Sam enough to have a pure honest conversation with him. Sam would have been understanding and would have helped him realize coming out is a process and an adventure that each must make alone. But with the help of others by their side as they decide how fast the process will go. It differs for each person.

Jean-Claude knew he loved Sam and finally decided to tell his family he was gay and he didn't care about the result. All he knew was he was tired of hiding that he was gay from his family. So one day Jean-Claude made a call back to Michigan. His stepmother answered the phone, "Hello?" Replying with his voice cracking Jean-Claude said, "Hi, this is Jean-Claude I need to tell you something." His stepmother without emotion said, "Oh yeah, okay." Jean-Claude just blurted it out, "I'm gay" and waited in silence for any number of responses that he had worked out in his head. Jean-Claude's stepmother said, "Well, we thought so a long time ago." Jean-Claude started to freak out thinking, "wait, you already knew this, what the hell?" His stepmother continued, "But there are some things that you need to know. Do not come home if you get AIDS and you will not say a word about this to your brother or sister, we will take care of it. I will let your grandparents know and you just do what you need to do and we will do the same." Jean-Claude thought, "What the fuck?!? What are you saying? Why are you telling anyone? Oh shit, I've really done it this time." By the tone in her voice Jean-Claude knew what was being said without the actual words being spoken: "Don't come home… don't talk to your brother or sister ever… we will talk to the family and we will decide your fate… you go live your life and stay out of ours." Jean-Claude knew better than to question anything because the wrath that would follow would be one that could not be stopped.

Jean-Claude's worst nightmare was about to begin. All communication with his family was cut off; no more letters, no phone calls, and no care packages – he was completely alone – the biggest fear that Jean-Claude had in his life. When in reality, if Jean-Claude had just taken a second, Sam was right there with nothing but love.

Sam tried to help Jean-Claude through his coming out, but it was of no use, Jean-Claude just closed himself off from everyone to protect himself from getting hurt. Jean-Claude began lashing out again destroying anything and everything in his path. The cycle had begun again.

"Oh my Chickie, over the telephone? Well I guess, you were in Germany, not like you could have flown home just to tell them now could you? But really, was this premeditated or did you just do it on a whim? Ms. Wauneta stopped what she was doing and looked directly at Jean-Claude awaiting a response. Jean-Claude responded, "It was on a wing and a prayer and just happened, I just reached my limits and felt I couldn't hide who I was any longer." "Ok, I understand; that might explain why you are so afraid of taking risks in life since between Sam and your parents they didn't turn out so well." Ms. Wauneta said as she rummaged through a dresser drawer.

The relationship between Sam and Jean-Claude took a turn one day when an alert was called. When an alert is called the entire Battalion must be out the gate Zulu plus 4 (the time the alert was called plus 4 hours). Some may have a difficult time understanding how they manage to move roughly 5,000 personnel, assigned weapons, gear, vehicles, ammunition and food in four hours. But it is accomplished in what can be referred to as organized chaos. When alert is called Jean-Claude immediately goes to the S-4 office and begins preparing: pulling codebooks from S-2 (Intelligence), obtaining plans from S-3 as well as movement instructions for the entire Battalion. Inventory of goods such as food, ammunition and fuel on hand must be obtained and orders for future needs must be planned before departure. Meanwhile Sam was off to the motor pool to grab the Humvee, load up both Jean-Claude's and his A bags, go to the armory to check out weapons for both Jean-Claude and himself, as well as getting chemical suits for both. There is a lot for him to carry out in a short period of time as well. Jean-Claude grabbed his checklist from the drawer and began going down the list. He reached the item "com check" and ran downstairs as they would be leaving soon, he asked Sam, "Have you performed a com check?" No response. Jean-Claude asked again, "Did you perform a com check?" Sam snapped, "No, and I don't need to either." Jean-Claude saw red and yelled, "You will do a com check because it is required before we can pull out." Sam glared at Jean-Claude and said, "Fuck you" and walked away. Jean-Claude was livid, "Sam get back here and do a com check because it is your responsibility." Sam turned around looked at Jean-Claude red in the face and said, "No, I will not, you can do it yourself, why do I have to do it anyway, we know it works." Jean-Claude was so angry all he could say was, "Because I said do it and it is an order." Sam, being equally angry, said, "Fine" and continued to say something under his breath that Jean-Claude didn't hear. It was best that Jean-Claude never heard what was said as it would have just intensified the situation beyond control.

Jean-Claude was angry because for the first time Sam fought back, he just chose the wrong time to fight back with Jean-Claude. Jean-Claude had been treating Sam like crap for a long time, to the point of ignoring him, going off doing his own thing, not putting Sam in front of his own feelings and Jean-Claude thought this was acceptable. Jean-Claude was also not happy of the fact that Sam chose to disobey him in a public fashion and on an alert as well; he felt Sam was not taking it seriously. What Jean-Claude thought had no bearing on why Sam chose that moment to fight back and lash out; Jean-Claude had this coming for a long time.

Everyone in the shop knew there was something going on between Sam and Jean-Claude because both of them were being sharp with each other during the entire alert exercise. Normally, Sam and Jean-Claude got along very well and never raised voices at each other. So the other guys in the shop tried to stay out of the line of fire to no avail, Jean-Claude was on a rampage with a scorched earth policy. Everyone in the shop got hit with something and Jean-Claude could be a real ass when he desired without putting much thought into it actually.

When the exercise was completed, equipment returned and it was finally time to go back to the room, neither Sam nor Jean-Claude would speak to each other. This went on for an entire week. Both Sam and Jean-Claude spent more and more time away from each other to avoid talking about what had happened. Finally, Jean-Claude spoke to Sam one night and asked if they could talk; he was not expecting what happened next. Sam went off, "You have been treating me like shit and I'm tired of it..." many things were said and Jean-Claude felt horrible, but hid those feelings and fought back. It was the only fight Sam and Jean-Claude ever had the entire time they were together, not that Jean-Claude did anything thing to help the situation, it was all Sam avoiding the fights. Jean-Claude deserved this tongue-lashing and all the bad feelings that went with it because he caused all these feelings in Sam to come out finally.

Sam and Jean-Claude went back to not talking for a few more days and then there was the weekend. Finally, they sat down and spoke to each other and cleared the air the best they could and piece back together the relationship. Sam knew exactly what he wanted and Jean-Claude had no clue what he wanted as he was so confused about things. Jean-Claude did the only thing he knew to save what he had with Sam, he became nice to Sam and settled down and stopped being a complete ass to Sam.

"Ah, that explains it, I always wondered." Ms. Wauneta said while looking at earrings. "Wondered what?" Jean-Claude asked. Ms. Wauneta quietly spoke "Why when someone raises their voice at you for any reason, you will go extremely quiet and the wheels start turning. Where your mind is taking you I don't know, but you get quiet very fast." With tears welling up, Jean-Claude said, "Because I get scared, I get scared of saying or doing something and the person will just go away. Especially if I care about them, I turn into this little boy needing acceptance and I just got scolded for acting up, because truly, most of the time, I am acting up and being a boob." "Well you said it Chickie, not me." Ms. Wauneta chuckled as she went about fidgeting with her body stuffing.

Another field exercise was coming up; this one was a big deal as the Battalion would be going out to qualify on weapons. The planning of this exercise had taken months to plan and everyone was looking forward to getting out of the barracks and into the field. Soldiers tend to get cabin fever when trapped in garrison too long.

So off to Howenfels they went. Jean-Claude went up as part of the advance party to get everything ready for the Battalion before they were due to arrive in mass five days later. Leaving the rest of the S-4 office behind Sam and Jean-Claude went to Howenfels. This exercise was going to have its share of problems, since the Battalion had pulled the rotation to stay in "tent city." This meant erecting GP large tents with a minimum number of people and working out billeting problems for armories, mess hall facilities among just a few. To make matters even worse, tent city was located right behind the tank qualifying range; providing a nuisance that could not be fixed.

While everyone was off setting up tents, Sam took time to put both his and Jean-Claude's gear inside a tent, set up cots and get ready for our long stay. When Jean-Claude went into the tent that night he saw that Sam had set the cots up in a very interesting position. As you entered the tent, Sam's cot was vertical next to the door and he had set up Jean-Claude's cot horizontal with the head of the cot closest to the head of his cot. Jean-Claude was so tired he didn't move the cots and they both went to sleep.

Finally, the rest of the Battalion started arriving in staggered convoys, with some vehicles not making it in until late at night as they broke down along the road on the way. If a vehicle breaks down it gets repaired and off they go again; but this means they are even more tired and hungry when they arrive. It can be a very long night for members of Battalion staff or the mess hall.

The thing that made it rough was the tanks qualifying at night as well and would be firing their huge cannons all night. So much so it was difficult to sleep and the cots would vibrate across the tent pad during the night. It was not uncommon to wake up in the middle of the night and find yourself waking up several feet from where you started the night. They finally staked down the cots so they could no longer travel across the tent. One night, Jean-Claude woke up and Sam's arm was laying down his side, he jumped out of bed and Mason was on fireguard at the time and saw Jean-Claude jump out of bed. Mason just looked at Jean-Claude, smiled and quietly said, "We have known for some time, don't worry about it."

"Don't worry about it! What the fuck?!" was all Jean-Claude could think; panic set in and Jean-Claude's mind started to race with all the horrible thoughts of what might happen to both he and Sam. Jean-Claude was in a world of hurt because not only was he with a guy, but a guy in his chain of command, this was a big deal. Now Mason had something to hang over Jean-Claude's head. It was full panic red-alert mode for Jean-Claude, he started acting out and getting real nasty with Sam; it was the only thing that Jean-Claude could do to dispel the rumors that he was gay. This was all so unfair to Sam and Sam put his foot down with Jean-Claude and asked, "Why are you treating me like shit again?" Jean-Claude pulled Sam close and whispered, "Mason knows about us." Sam just grinned and said, "I figured he knew. I don't care, I will get kicked out for love." Jean-Claude looked at Sam in complete disbelief; he was thinking, "How can you just give everything up for love?" Jean-Claude's brain was short circuiting over this statement. "How can he be so confident about who he is?" Jean-Claude thought and finally looking at Sam in complete despair he said, "I need to get away." Again, Jean-Claude ran away from the situation and the man that was madly in love with him to be alone.

"Oh my friggin' God, you boob! Sometimes I swear you don't have the sense God gave a mouse. This guy was completely in love with you and it didn't matter who or what the circumstances; he was going to be there for you." Ms. Wauneta exclaimed poking Jean-Claude in the chest. "I know, I know, now, but I didn't know that then!" Jean-Claude tried to defend himself. "No excuse, sometimes I swear you cannot see the forest through the trees Jean-Claude." Ms. Wauneta screeched and she went back to getting ready.

Jean-Claude walked toward the motor pool in a daze. He didn't know what to think or do, his secret was out and there was no way to get it back in the bottle. Jean-Claude started feeling nauseous, shaky and he just wanted to hide and cry. Jean-Claude somehow gained control over his feelings and thought, "It can be controlled, no problem, act as if nothing happened and keep going." The art of compartmentalization took hold and into the box everything went to deal with another day.

The relationship between Jean-Claude and Sam was strained, at best, because Sam didn't know how to get to Jean-Claude and get him to talk about things. It certainly was not from a lack of trying, every time Sam tried to get close, Jean-Claude would push him away. Jean-Claude's thought process was one of self-preservation at all costs. Jean-Claude didn't take Sam's feelings into consideration at all.

All of Jean-Claude's actions were pushing Sam to his breaking point. Jean-Claude was destroying any chance of a lasting relationship with Sam; all because he was scared of just letting go and relying on Sam and just falling in love. Jean-Claude needed to trust and believe Sam was only going to what was best for the both of them; but this was beyond Jean-Claude's grasp.

Returning to the States

The time was coming for Jean-Claude's tour of duty to end as well as he needed to decide if he was going to sign up for another contract with the Army or get out. Jean-Claude spent many nights wrestling with this decision. Jean-Claude was struggling with the knowledge he would not see Sam any longer. It was going to be another Brad situation all over again. Jean-Claude felt lost and alone and there was no one that he would allow to help him through his next choice.

Finally, Jean-Claude decided to exit the Army. There was no rhyme or reason how he arrived at the decision, but one reason was the question on the reenlistment papers, "Have you had any homosexual encounter?" He would have to lie and Jean-Claude didn't think he could make it past that question. Also, Sam was not around much and was spending much time with a Writer friend that he had made. Jean-Claude didn't want anything to do with the Writer because he knew a few of the things that Sam was saying to him. Jean-Claude didn't trust the Writer and felt betrayed by Sam for even saying anything about their relationship to anyone.

Sam was treating Jean-Claude like crap and all Jean-Claude could do was try to be as nice as possible. Sam was hurting Jean-Claude at the core and not caring; "Can't really blame him for treating me this way" Jean-Claude thought. "I deserve anything he dishes out," Jean-Claude thought and decided to just take whatever Sam thought was fitting. Jean-Claude didn't care how often he felt like crap or how guilty he felt for treating Sam they way he did; he could not discuss it with Sam. When Jean-Claude was alone in the room and knew Sam would be gone he would just sit and cry. Finally, Jean-Claude concluded, "I deserve to feel bad about this and I don't deserve Sam anyway, so move on with life."

This all sounded good in theory, but every time Jean-Claude saw Sam his chest would tighten and the feelings of guilt would wash over his body. From the outside looking in, no one would have any idea Jean-Claude was going through so much turmoil, Jean-Claude had become extremely artful at hiding his feelings. If anyone even got close to getting Jean-Claude to talk about his feelings; Jean-Claude would deflect the question and begin controlling the conversation away from his feelings.

> "Chickie, you still do that! Remember the first time we met? I alluded to you that my friend Brent liked you and you quickly changed the subject?" Ms. Wauneta said looking down at Jean-Claude.

It was the beginning of September; Jean-Claude was now less than 30 days out from leaving Germany. Jean-Claude started pulling back from his duties in S-4 and was seeing Sam less and less. Jean-Claude became obsessed with clearing Germany to make the timetable to transfer out of the Army. There were so many appointments to keep. From cleaning all the gear for return, to washing everything and piling it up for the German packers to come in and box everything up for transport back to the States. On top of all of this, the Battalion was preparing to go back out to the field for 45 days. So Jean-Claude was splitting his time between clearing and preparing the guys to go out to the field as he would not be joining them this time; he would be staying behind. This brought some sadness to Jean-Claude as he started thinking of what he was going to miss.

Then the day came, it was time for the Battalion to move out to the field. Jean-Claude did everything he normally did when the Battalion was moving out; except for one part…he stood there watching as they drove off. Jean-Claude was alone now, it was quiet, and he slowly turned to begin walking to his room as there was no work to be done. He went to bed and just cried. The pain in his chest was crushing; the sadness of never seeing Sam again came blaring into his head. "The next eight days were going to be hell" Jean-Claude thought, "I don't have much clearing left and that won't take too long, can't watch TV since that was packed a couple of days ago. What am I going to do?"

Jean-Claude filled his days with clearing, goofing off, going to the bowling alley, drinking and just feeling sorry for himself. Jean-Claude finally sat down and began writing a letter to leave on Sam's bed so he would get it when he returned from the field. The letter almost turned into a short story as Jean-Claude just kept writing his feelings down and pouring everything out on the pages in front of him. Finally the letter was completed and he laid it on Sam's bed. Now there were only three days to go until Jean-Claude would be leaving for Ft. Dix to out-process.

It was Jean-Claude' last full day in Germany, just needed to wake up tomorrow and he was on a plane to the States. Jean-Claude decided to walk down to Jaeger Kaserne and goof off, stop to have a cappuccino at his favorite street café and relax. On his return to Graves Kaserne; Jean-Claude was walking past Battalion Headquarters when he saw the S-4 VW panel van. Jean-Claude thought, "Oh, they must be making the mail run, no use asking who it is because the S-4 crew is shorthanded and they wouldn't be allowed back here." He continued on up the hill to his room. As Jean-Claude entered the room there was a noise of rustling paper; it was Sam, he had the letter Jean-Claude had written in his hand. Jean-Claude froze and just looked at Sam in amazement, "How did you get back here?" he asked. Sam grinned and said, "I planned this and worked it out with the guys for me to come back and I'll be spending the night here. I wanted to be with you on your last night here." Jean-Claude didn't know what to think, he was overcome with joy at seeing Sam and it was like nothing had ever happened for that very moment.

Sam was quick to point Jean-Claude's attention to the letter he had written. "Do you mean this what you wrote?" he asked. Jean-Claude looked down at the floor and quietly said, "Yes, I love you and I'm sorry for the stuff I've done. Can you forgive me?" Sam, in his usual manner said, "Yes, I've been waiting for you to say these things." Jean-Claude fell into Sam's arms and he didn't want to let go, he never wanted this to end.

Sam started talking, "Well what we need to do is figure out how we are going to stay together. How many days will you be at Ft. Dix?" "Five." Jean-Claude responded. "Okay, then you can go live with my sister in New York. Give her a call when you know when your flight to New York and she will come pick you up at the airport." Sam said with an air of confidence that Jean-Claude had always been jealous of because it was a weakness of his. With that being settled, Jean-Claude and Sam fell into one last night of passion in Germany. Snuggling together in the single bed together and sleeping tightly all night in each other's arms. This last night together will be seared into Jean-Claude's mind forever. Sam this massive 180 pound man with a large chest and arms and Jean-Claude a slender 120 pound man in a single bed, turning in unison through the night and neither waking up, it was so natural and pure. For one night, it was just Sam and Jean-Claude no one else, nothing to worry about, nothing to plan for, nothing fear, just pure love.

The next morning Sam had to take off early as he had gotten permission to stay the night when he should have been back in the field and they were waiting for him. Jean-Claude felt his chest tighten as Sam drove off, but he didn't have much time himself to think of things, he needed to get ready to travel to the airport and head to the States.

Growing Up in a Tiny Town

Younger Years

Jean-Claude's earliest memories were around three years old; they are just glimpses and images, but seemed to have had a profound effect on his life. His first memory is being shoved into his room and hearing the lock click in the door. He was locked inside his bedroom; he started to cry and he heard, "Shut up before I give you something to cry about." Jean-Claude settled down and started playing with his toys. He had no idea how long he was in the room, but he had to go to the bathroom and started yelling for his mother; no response. Jean-Claude finally gave up and peed in his sand pail by the door and went back to playing. Jean-Claude looked up at the door to the sound of the lock being pulled and his mother entered, looked at the pail and yanked Jean-Claude up and began hitting him. Jean-Claude squirmed with all his might to get away, but she had a firm hold on him.

The next memory is an odd one, even for Jean-Claude: it is Easter and Jean-Claude is roaming the house looking for hidden eggs to put in his basket. He spots one up on the hanging lamp in the flu, it is his favorite color blue and he wants it bad. He looks at his mother for help and she laughed.

Another memory is being told to put the Spaghetti-O can on the counter and when his mother went into the kitchen she started yelling and coming after him. Jean-Claude ran out the back door and dove into the large doghouse in the backyard. The family St. Bernard sat down in front of the door. Jean-Claude stayed in there while his mother yelled and didn't come out. Jean-Claude remembers his dad pulling him out of the doghouse and it being dark.

A memory carried with him every day is when his mother was mad and slammed the car door before Jean-Claude could get his hand out of the way and he caught his thumb in the door. Jean-Claude forever has one thumb smaller and fatter than the other.

Jean-Claude has several memories of strange men in the house when his dad was gone. They would call him 'buddy, ' 'champ, ' 'little guy' and invariably asked to be called uncle something or other. Jean-Claude hated these men and they always liked to pat him on the head. As Jean-Claude grew up, he hated anyone touching his head or making a motion like they would touch him.

The final memory of his mother is coming home with his dad after spending the day with his grandparents and walking into the house and everything inside was gone; the house was completely bare and his mother was gone. His dad turned around and put Jean-Claude back into the car and loaded up the dog and they returned to his grandparents where they lived for some time. Later Jean-Claude would learn his parents had gotten divorced. Jean-Claude never saw his biological mother again; she simply disappeared.

Jean-Claude was five years old and had been put in school at four; his dad worked all the time and needed a baby-sitter. Jean-Claude remembers the first time he saw Roda; she was short, big butt, red hair and blue eyes; and she didn't like the St. Bernard. Jean-Claude was forever riding the St. Bernard around the trailer park and he was always getting in trouble for it because Roda couldn't find him. Jean-Claude just thought of this as a game and a challenge to disappear whenever he could.

Jean-Claude and his dad were forming a strong bond since it was just the two 'bachelors" as Uncle Butch put it. Jean-Claude got to ride on the motorcycle all the time with his dad. Jean-Claude would always fall asleep on the back of the bike resting his head on his dad's back and holding on. Or the car trips all over town in the purple Gremlin which Jean-Claude called the "purple people eater."

Stepmother

Jean-Claude remembers when his dad started seeing Roda all the time, they would go out on dates. Eventually they were going to be married and on the night of the rehearsal, dinner while sitting in the backseat, Jean-Claude called out, "Roda." She turned around and said, "After tomorrow you will have to call me mom." Jean-Claude just stared back at her while she continued, "I mean it, no more Roda it is mom."

Looking back Jean-Claude always smirks at this memory because it was the beginning of the battle of wills in his mind between his stepmother and him. At the wedding they had put him in a beige suit with a bright blue tie; Jean-Claude hated the tie and kept pulling at it. And at the reception, he kept getting in the way and tried to get into as many pictures that he could with his finger up his nose. Oh yes, the war had begun. When the photos came in from the wedding, Jean-Claude got a good beating from his stepmother; she was livid.

Shortly after their wedding they were moving out to the country next to his step-grandparents. As a wedding gift they had given two acres and proceeded building a house. On the day they were moving, Jean-Claude went outside to get the St. Bernard but he wasn't in the backyard. As he turned to shout his stepmother was on the stairs and said, "We are not taking your dog; we found him another home." Jean-Claude said, "That ok I guess." Jean-Claude was boiling inside he hated this evil witch and all he could think of was the story of Cinderella and the evil step-mother. Jean-Claude didn't cry, yell or beg, he simply walked past her, got into the backseat of the car and folded his arms and waited to go.

The town where they moved to was considered a "village" and consisted of roughly 1,300 residents. Everyone knew everyone and what everyone was doing at any given time. It was a village where the main sport was gossiping about other people and what they were doing. If a person didn't comply with the "image" of what one should be doing, it flew through the town and within 24-hours everyone knew about it. The town consisted of one of everything: one police officer; one pharmacy; one grocery store; one feed store; one barber; one library; one church; one hairdresser; one playground; one dentist, etc. The main intersection was a flashing yellow light; it didn't even rate a "red, yellow, green" light. Really, how fast could a tractor go through town? It was not unusual to see a horse tied to the parking meters as people conducted business. It was from growing up here; Jean-Claude became a very private person, do not say anything to anyone for fear it would spread throughout the town and all your business would be out in the street. Jean-Claude applied this to his life and fiercely guarded information.

Jean-Claude was about to turn seven and he was visiting his grandparents in the neighboring town with his parents and his cousin Miles was there as well from Florida. Miles was a nice guy that played with Jean-Claude outside. While they were playing hide-and-seek, Miles hid in some bushes next to the shed far in the back of the yard out of sight of everyone. When Jean-Claude finally found him Miles pulled Jean-Claude into the bushes with him and started hugging him. Jean-Claude felt good resting against Miles' chest. Miles started running his hands all over Jean-Claude's body and spending much time on his crotch. Miles guided Jean-Claude's hand to his crotch and Jean-Claude was surprised to find it was hard. Miles pulled down Jean-Claude's pants and took his penis into his mouth; Jean-Claude had never felt anything like this. Miles kept sucking on him and Jean-Claude started getting a funny feeling down there and started peeing on Miles. Miles said, "Go ahead, it is okay." Then Miles unzipped his pants and asked Jean-Claude, "Now you can do me like that." Jean-Claude reached into Miles' pants and pulled out his adult penis and put it into his mouth. Jean-Claude

94

kept sucking and Miles was moaning and he pulled out and white stuff spurted all over Jean-Claude's face. Miles looked down at him and said, "What a dirty boy, look what you made me do to you. You liked sucking on that didn't you? This is our secret don't tell anyone because if you do they will take you away." Jean-Claude nodded his head in understanding while Miles was cleaning off his face. Jean-Claude never spoke of this to anyone and went back to the house and sat quietly at the table waiting to go home.

Jean-Claude had just turned nine and was getting ready to go to bed on his birthday. As with any other night, Jean-Claude changed into his pajamas and went to the living room, where dad was doing the crossword puzzle, to give him a kiss good night. Jean-Claude got halfway across the living room and his stepmother said, "I think you need to stop that, you are too old to be kissing your father good night, go to your room." Jean-Claude just looked at his dad then his stepmother and back again. "What did I say," his stepmother said. Jean-Claude turned quickly and headed down the hall. Jean-Claude climbed into bed and started to cry, he felt his dad had been taken away from him. He was angry at her for taking him away; she would regret this.

Jean-Claude started acting up something fierce and was getting spankings regularly for several months after the living room incident. Jean-Claude would look for things that would make his stepmother mad, full well knowing he was going to get in trouble. He didn't care and the spankings didn't hurt any more, even the belt didn't hurt, he no longer cried when getting hit. One day he went too far when broke a dish goofing around in the kitchen, his stepmother came around the corner quickly and grabbed his forearm and sunk her nails into his flesh. This brought Jean-Claude to a dead stop because it hurt really badly. She realized she had gotten Jean-Claude's attention and this would become the standard form of punishment.

As Jean-Claude got older he became extremely adept at the game he like to refer to as "The Big Red Button." The goal was to see how many times he could push his stepmother's button before she would explode in anger and start yelling. He was never allowed to go anywhere besides school and the farm for chores so this became his form of entertainment. It was soon after he turned 12 that he learned the art of looking at items in a room, on a shelf and memorizing exactly how everything looked. This came in handy when he was sneaking food so he wouldn't get caught even though all he had to do was ask and the food would have been given. Jean-Claude never wanted to ask for anything from someone because it could be taken away. Jean-Claude also learned how to eavesdrop without getting caught as well. This proved extremely useful because he was learning just how his games were working on his stepmother as she would talk on the phone to her mother about what Jean-Claude was doing to her.

At 13 something happened with Jean-Claude, he simply stopped talking as much and found comfort in books. He didn't get along with anyone at school and kept to himself all the time. Jean-Claude did his chores, his homework and read his books. He found if he just followed the program it was easier. However, the second child arrived and Jean-Claude was put in charge of his little brother Kyle who was three. This was a whole new set of responsibilities which Jean-Claude kept getting yelled at for one thing or another and those claws of his stepmother's would come out into his arm. Jean-Claude began spending every moment he could get away outside far away from the house and would not go back until he absolutely had to go back. During the winter months he would huddle next to the fireplace around the corner where no one could see him and hide there for hours; not wanting to go inside.

Either Jean-Claude just gave up or he learned how to maneuver around his family to avoid confrontations. He started feeling oppressed and no matter what he wanted to do was always told "no;" so he just finally gave up. As he got older his stepmother asked if he was interested in sports and wanted to join any leagues. Jean-Claude immediately replied, "No, I'm not interested in those things." However, the one sport he was very interested in was volleyball, but because the school only had a woman's team and he knew he would not be allowed to play. The other item was that he just didn't want to be bothered with the "strings" that would be attached to him wanting to do something. This way if he didn't want anything there was nothing that could be controlled by another person.

Birthdays and Christmas would come and go and each year the adults would ask what he wanted for gifts and every time the reply would be the same, "Nothing." Jean-Claude's thinking was, "if you didn't ask for anything they could never hold it over your head or take it away. It is better to just keep away." As Jean-Claude got older, this thought process was consuming his life and it seemed to him to be a very efficient way of dealing with things.

For Jean-Claude's stepmother image was extremely important. For example, there was a time when Jean-Claude was headed to the barn to do chores and on the way out his stepmother looked at him and said, "You are not going out the door without your belt, go get it on. What will people think if they see you?" This would be a normal exercise whenever he was going outside the house, he would get the once over from his stepmother every time. This became part of Jean-Claude's life and every time he got dressed he thought, "Image is everything." It was so engrained that Jean-Claude wouldn't go out the front door to pick up the paper without being presentably dressed.

Jean-Claude was trying to get his stepmother's attention while his stepmother was in the kitchen cooking with his aunt and grandma. After several attempts to get her to respond by calling her "mom" he raised his voice and said, "Mother." His stepmother immediately took the three steps toward him, slapped him across the face hard enough to turn his head and said, "I know exactly what you meant by that." Jean-Claude glared at her wanting to say, "Really, you do, you fucking bitch" but he just turned and headed outside. Once away from the house he started talking out loud to himself: "Who does she think she is hitting me like that? That will be the last time she ever hits me, next time I will hit her back. God, I cannot wait to get out of here!"

When Jean-Claude went back to the house he refused to look at anyone or speak to anyone, even if they asked him a direct question, he simply looked at them not saying a word. This lasted for two entire weeks and finally people just stopped talking to him; at last Jean-Claude was happy – he was being left alone.

High School

In high school Jean-Claude was put into the advanced classes and he would always drag every single book home from school each night to study, "whether he had homework or not" because this is what his stepmother demanded. Jean-Claude got good grades and was quiet in school and kept to himself, he felt he just didn't fit in with anyone.

One day as Jean-Claude was getting ready for gym class at his regular locker, Jean-Claude noticed this boy Tom took the locker next to his. This seemed strange to Jean-Claude because Tom normally took a locker all the way at the other end with the cool kids. As Jean-Claude was crouched down tying his shoes Tom called his name and as he looked up and tried to say, "What" Tom shoved his dick into Jean-Claude's mouth. Jean-Claude pulled back and looked around; there was no one in the locker room beside him and Tom. Tom just laughed and said, "I knew you would like that, you will have to suck me off sometime." Jean-Claude looked down and he was hard as rock; this encounter had turned him on; now he had to wait before he could go out into the gym. Tom never came around to collect on his statement and Jean-Claude avoided him at all cost anyway.

Jean-Claude figured out Tom's schedule and his movements around school so it wasn't too difficult to avoid him.

Another incident was the school bully kept going after Jean-Claude day after day. He told the principal and all he got was, "deal with it that is high school." Jean-Claude tried to avoid this guy because he was just so mean and everyone would follow his lead. Not even a week after the incident with Tom; the school bully started calling Jean-Claude a fag. This made Jean-Claude very angry. The "fag" comments kept coming every day and it was spreading to other people. Jean-Claude tolerated this for six agonizing weeks. Finally, late one day after school, as Jean-Claude was heading to drama practice the bully said, "Hey fag, suck on anything lately?" Jean-Claude stopped dropped his books and shoved the bully backwards falling down the two flights of the grand staircase. Jean-Claude left him lying on the floor and went to practice not telling anyone what had happened.

Jean-Claude figured he was in real deep trouble when he got home because news traveled so fast around town. A big rule in his family was no physical fighting. When he got home he was dreading going into the house. When he entered the house was quiet and he quickly darted off to his room to change clothes and head to the farm to do chores. At dinner Jean-Claude was waiting for the yelling to begin, but to his surprise, nothing. Jean-Claude waited weeks to get in trouble, but the subject was never discussed. Jean-Claude finally let his concerns go thinking, "the bully must not have said a word either."

The only after-school activity Jean-Claude participated in was drama. He loved doing plays and hiding behind a made up character. Learning the lines was easy for Jean-Claude, as he just pretended to be this whole new person and enjoyed getting out of his life for some time. The school was doing a production of Brigadoon and at the last minute the person playing a major player got ill; Jean-Claude volunteered to learn the part and perform in less than 24 hours. Looking back makes Jean-Claude chuckle; there were cue cards all over the place with his lines, including the backs of other players. His parents never attended a single play that he performed. However, they never missed a little league game for his little brother and sister. Jean-Claude took this personally and withdrew further within himself.

Around his sophomore year in high school, Jean-Claude would fantasize about the day he finally got to leave this tiny town and get away from his family. He knew that he would get out of here and never come back as soon as he got the chance. Once away from his family he could do whatever he wanted and not have to worry of being oppressed and hiding his emotions and feelings.

The summer before senior year he had made friends with the kid down the road, Dan. Dan was 6'1", short black hair, brown eyes, soft olive skin fit from lifting weights and a huge package. Jean-Claude and he would go horseback riding and hang out at each other's farms. One day when Jean-Claude was at Dan's they were hanging out in the hayloft. Dan had decided to wear a pair of tight fitting green shorts and tennis shoes, nothing else. Dan and Jean-Claude took a walk around talking about different things and at one point were sitting on the fence of the covered pens and Jean-Claude was staring at Dan's huge package. Dan caught him and said, "Would you stop staring." Jean-Claude turned beet red and made up an excuse to get out of there as fast as he could. Jean-Claude didn't really give what just happened much thought.

As the senior year progressed, Jean-Claude had to start thinking about what to do after school was completed. His stepmother made it perfectly clear that after graduation he had to do something, anything. His stepmother continually drove it home by asking, "So have you decided what you are going to do? Remember, you can't stay here if you don't have a job and are paying rent." Jean-Claude always dreaded this conversation because it always ended with the same lecture, "You can't continue to stay here and be a deadbeat, we did our job raising you, now you need to do something on your own."

One day Jean-Claude saw a guy in a green uniform approaching the school, he waved and the solder waived back. Jean-Claude was curious so he followed to see where he was going. After seeing he went into the main office; Jean-Claude entered right behind him and went around the counter. Jean-Claude volunteered with the front office every day, so he was allowed full access to the office. He went and sat down at the far desk and was listening to the secretary's conversation with the soldier: "Sure, we can set something up to meet the kids to sign them up for information. When would be a good time for you? The soldier replied, "Anytime is good, you just let me know and we will be here." Jean-Claude interrupted, "what information?" The soldier turned and looked at Jean-Claude and said, "Would you be interested in going into the Army to travel and learn a skill?" Jean-Claude heard 'travel' and was hooked; he could get out of this little town and away from his family.

> Ms. Wauneta patted Jean-Claude on the head and said, "Chickie, at some point was all come from a Podunk town someplace, even if they come from a big city. Some have it a little rougher than others like you did and they do anything to get away. So you chose the Army as your way out. It could be worse, you could still be stuck there you know."

Enlisting in Guard/Army

Jean-Claude decided; he was going to enlist in the National Guard. At dinner one night he told his parents of his decision and waited for the response. There was silence until his stepmother said, "What are you thinking?" in her shrill manner. His dad stopped eating and just stared at Jean-Claude. His dad finally quietly said, "Go to your room, we will call you out when we are ready to discuss this decision."

Jean-Claude got up from the table and dropped off his plate in the sink on his way to his room. As Jean-Claude sat waiting to be called back out, he started doing his homework, not really thinking of what might be coming. He had decided and there was no changing his mind. Glancing at the clock Jean-Claude made a note that it had been two hours since being sent to his room. "Hmm, this must be eating at them. Good." he thought.

Finally he was called back out and his dad started, "I don't agree with your decision and I want to meet with the recruiter and ask some of my own questions." Jean-Claude calmly said, "Okay, I will set up the meeting." Jean-Claude glanced over at his stepmother and she was grinding her teeth and just glaring at him. Jean-Claude chuckled to himself and thought, "Oh, she is pissed, and she knows there is nothing she can do about it. She has lost control and she doesn't like it. What did she think was going to happen, she kept saying I had to do something."

The following week on Friday night the recruiter showed up at the house promptly at the scheduled time. Jean-Claude's dad wasted no time grilling the recruiter: "Does he get to choose his occupation? What guarantees can you provide that he stays in that occupation and the military doesn't change it? How long is the contract? What is the training like?" The questions just kept coming for hours until finally his dad stopped and asked Jean-Claude, "Do you understand everything that we discussed?" "Yes Sir, I do." Jean-Claude's dad looked at him for a while and said, "Well then you can sign the contract. What do you need from me?" The recruiter quickly opened a folder and pulled out a waiver form for Jean-Claude's dad to sign because Jean-Claude was only 16 when he entered into the contract. Basic training would be put off until after graduation, but Jean-Claude could start attending weekend drills with his unit and earning time in grade.

Once the contracts were signed that evening Jean-Claude went to bed feeling happy because he was getting out of this town and away from his family. On Monday when he went to school his classmates were asking questions about signing up for the Army. Once again, his stepmother's big mouth had struck again.

Graduation was only a couple of weeks away and Jean-Claude was excited at the prospects of starting a new life away from this place. Jean-Claude started boxing up his things to be stored in the basement since his parents were going to have Kyle move into his room when he left for the Army. It was during one of these packing sessions the door to his room opened up and his dad stood in the doorway. Jean-Claude jumped, his dad never came to his room. Jean-Claude's dad said, "We need to take a walk."

Jean-Claude followed his dad outside to the shed, where his dad spent a lot of time puttering around fixing cars. His dad said, "Pull up a chair," while handing him a yellow envelope. "In that envelope are your birth certificate and the divorce papers between your mother and I. I will answer any question you have this one time only and we will never speak of it again." Jean-Claude looked at his dad in shock while opening the envelope. Jean-Claude said, "I have one question, why did she leave us all alone dad?" Jean-Claude's dad sighed and looked at the floor saying, "Well she let us down. She was sleeping around and not taking good care of you and I couldn't let that happen. Betrayal of a person's trust is a serious offense." Jean-Claude just nodded and said, "I understand. We did okay though when it was just us dad." His dad's head shot up and he stared at Jean-Claude with the look Jean-Claude knew well, he had crossed a line. "What do you mean by that statement?" he asked. Jean-Claude gulped and replied, "You did the best you could and we were fine until you gave me a stepmother with the same stuff going on. Do you know how many beatings I've had over the years? Do you know she digs her nails into my arms all the time? I don't like her." His dad replied in a dead tone as he stood up walking away, "That is your opinion, we are finished."

Jean-Claude was shaking after the encounter; he had never spoken to his dad with such distain. However, Jean-Claude was happy he had finally spoke up for himself and let his dad know how he felt.

Basic Training

Three days after graduation there was a government car in the driveway to take him to Detroit for in-processing. Jean-Claude said his goodbyes, stuck his one bag he was allowed in the trunk and they were off to pick up two other guys enlisting. They finally arrived at a flea infested hotel in Detroit late in the evening and were given a room and told they needed to get some sleep because they would be starting at 0300. Jean-Claude thought, "Who gets up at three in the morning?"

At exactly 0300 the door was tossed open, lights turned on and the occupants told, "You have 30 minutes to wash, dressed, packed and downstairs for breakfast. "Ugh, I'm still tired," Jean-Claude said out loud. After breakfast everyone piled into buses and headed off to the processing station. It was exactly like you see in the movies, drop your pants, turn your head and cough and move along to the next station. Around five in the afternoon, Jean-Claude was standing in a room filled with recruits taking his pledge. He was in the Army now.

Immediately after the officer said, "Welcome to the Army gentlemen" the doors flew open and sergeants began barking orders. Lucky for Jean-Claude and the time he had spend with his Guard unit, he knew how to deal with it; others not so well and Jean-Claude started to laugh, "Just do what they say and stay clear of them." he was thinking.

Immediately Jean-Claude was put on a bus heading for the airport. Off the bus, stand in line, get a ticket, go to the gate, and get on the plane for New York. At New York Jean-Claude got off the plan and looked at his book of tickets and found his next gate where, again, on the plane and off to Atlanta. In Atlanta off the plane, find the gate location to another waiting plane heading to Ft. Worth, Texas. Get off the plane in Ft. Worth and head out to the tarmac to a dinky little crop duster, squeeze in and get ready. As they headed up into the air the plane was bouncing all over the place and Jean-Claude thought he was going to be sick. When they finally landed, Jean-Claude was white as a ghost and thrilled to be off that flight. Jean-Claude grabbed his bag and headed to the front door where he saw two men in BDUs. He checked in and was told to get on the green bus outside and wait; it was 2330 at night.

They finally arrived at Ft. Sill in-processing unit at 0200 in the morning. A burly drill instructor got on the bus and started yelling, "Welcome to my Army girls, you have two minutes to get off my bus by any means possible except the windows starting now." Everyone flew down the aisle pushing and shoving to get off the bus. Once outside there were more drill instructors yelling instructions, the trick was to pick one drill instructor to listen to him and go with it. After initial in-processing, mainly searching for contraband and reviewing the personnel files they were sent to bed; it was 0500 a.m.

> "Ha, I remember those first few days in the Navy
> I wanted to smash the instructors over the head."
> Ms. Wauneta said with a reflective look on her
> face.

Wake up was 0830. Jean-Claude had never been this tired before and went through the motions in a daze. Haircuts were next on the menu and off they went to get shaved heads. Then off to uniforms, gear issued inoculation shots, eye exams, medical clearance, and Army field manuals. Three days later several of them were put on a bus and were taken to their actual basic training company.

Initially Jean-Claude was assigned to Third Platoon, but something happened and he was traded over to First Platoon. The lead Drill Instructor took a look at Jean-Claude and said, "Get over here mouse." Jean-Claude ran up and said, Yes Drill Sergeant." "Go to the third floor and stand by the door and wait for us." Jean-Claude grabbed his equipment and headed up the stairs. Soon the rest of the platoon was entering the billets.

Jean-Claude was stationed in what they called "New Hollywood" barracks. They were all brand new, clean and shiny with air-conditioning; most barracks on base did not have air-conditioning so they were lucky, especially as summer wore on and the heat just kept coming. The Drill Sergeant entered and said, "Mouse that will be your name while you are here with me. Your bunk is this one," pointing to a bunk right outside an office door. Jean-Claude tossed his gear on the bunk and began unpacking when he heard the Drill yell from inside the office, "Mouse, get in here." Jean-Claude just figured out what he was going to be doing most of basic training; he was going to be a runner for the Drill Instructor. This position came with a lot of privileges and Jean-Claude was happy and felt needed and a little special.

Jean-Claude hated going to the chow hall, for one reason was that because they thought he was too small the Army saw fit to place him on double rations. This didn't work to the Army's advantage; Jean-Claude never gained a single pound while in basic. The other reason he hated the chow hall was the way they had to line up to get food...it was, as the Drills' called it "Dick to ass" formation. Literally, you would stand so close to the guy in front of you that your dick was in his ass. When everyone was all hot and sweaty was the worse.

However, there was one time during the "Dick to ass" formation Jean-Claude had a bit of a surprise. As Jean-Claude moved from attention to parade rest the guy behind him moved forward and his dick was in Jean-Claude's hands. Jean-Claude thought it odd and moved slightly forward to get this guy's dick out of his hand. However, every time they took a step forward the guy would place his dick against Jean-Claude's hand. Then the guy started pushing against Jean-Claude's had and Jean-Claude realized the guy was hard! Jean-Claude kept hoping no one would notice and just keep looking forward.

Basic was the typical basic training and two days before graduation the Drill Instructor called him into the office and said, "Congratulations, you have graduated at the top of your class. You will be in the lead position in the formation for special recognition." Jean-Claude was proud; he was making something of himself without the help of anyone else. On graduation Jean-Claude got stuck in a "holding pattern." He could not go to Ft. Jackson because he had to wait for the next class cycle. Jean-Claude spent the next two weeks sleeping in and goofing off while the guys from his basic training unit were attending AIT. Jean-Claude was a supply clerk that for some reason was assigned to an artillery basic training – go figure.

AIT was uneventful, get up go to school, go home, study, and repeat. The only exception was Jean-Claude was allowed to have free time on Saturday and Sunday which he spent much time at the recreation hall down the street watching movies. If Jean-Claude had the opportunity, he got away from people.

As Jean-Claude's confidence grew with his performance in the military. Jean-Claude started making the change from introverted to opening his extroverted side; he found internal power in the idea that he would no longer be a victim and that he was in control. No one could hurt him and he should keep everyone at an arms distance seemed worked best for him.

Return to the States

Fort Dix – Choices

The flight back to the states was a nightmare flight. The plane was packed to capacity on the military flight. To make matters even worse, on the screen where normally movies would be showing was a map of Europe and the United States with a little plan and a red line showing the progress. Jean-Claude looked at that thing several times and concluded, "We are not moving at all just flying around in circles."

Suddenly Jean-Claude woke up as the plane was descending; he quickly looked out the window to see nothing but snow. "Where the hell are we?" Jean-Claude thought when just at that precise moment the captain came over the speakers, "We will be landing to take on fuel. During this process everyone must get off the plane and go inside the terminal. I also need to see the senior NCO on deck up front please." The NCO across the aisle from Jean-Claude stood up and headed to the cockpit.

The flight had approximately 200 soldiers returning to the US for different reasons and of the 200 there were 12 NCOs; Jean-Claude being one of them since he was a Corporal. The senior NCO returned and advised all the NCOs the status report: "We are to get all personnel directly from the plane to the terminal and keep them in formation facing the outer wall." The NCOs started to look at each other with the look of "what is the real deal here?" Senior NCO continued, "There is a Russian plane landing directly behind us to refuel as well and they will take their troops inside and we don't need an international incident." "Ah, now everything makes sense now." Jean-Claude thought.

Following the instructions of the Senior NCO, the soldiers exited the plan and faced the wall in formation with the

NCOs in the aisle to monitor the situation. Ten minutes later Jean-Claude heard the footsteps of marching troops as the Russians arrived; they did the same thing the U.S. did, placing their troops in formation facing the opposite wall with NCOs in the center watching. A couple of soldiers turned their heads and were met with a quick, "Turn around."

The plane landed at exactly time they had departed from Germany on the same day in New York. (Because of the time difference and the International Date Line, coming back to the States you essentially repeat an entire day.) For Jean-Claude that meant the out processing unit where he would spend the next five days. On arrival, bunks were assigned and brief instructions on how the process works and where they would be starting off in the morning.

Since everyone was still on German time everyone was up at 0300 and starting the day. Out processing was a complete daze for Jean-Claude; things were happening so fast and furious he could barely keep up and by late morning was tired. On the fourth day, Jean-Claude had to go to the travel office and advise them of his final destination since the Army was going to pay for a one-way ticket wherever he wanted. Jean-Claude asked the Sergeant if he could have some time to think about it and she said, "Yes."

Jean-Claude headed out the door and down the hall to get outside. Jean-Claude started to walk; he had no idea where he was going he just knew he needed to be alone. In the rain Jean-Claude started thinking in his head; "Do I go to New York where Sam wanted me to live with his sister or do I go to California and meet with Todd and start a life out there." All of a sudden Jean-Claude was panicking; "How can I live with Sam's sister. What am I going to do for work? I can't handle this."

Jean-Claude immediately went back to the travel office and said, "Send me to San Francisco please." With that one sentence a choice was made that would alter the course of his relationship with Sam and his entire life. Jean-Claude went to the pay phone in the hallway and called Sam's sister to advise her that he was going to California. Jean-Claude had no clue how this decision was going to impact his life.

"What?! You ass, what the hell were you thinking? You had just put the relationship back together after making a terrible mess of everything and Sam was giving you all his love on a silver platter. You decided to go to California?!? I ask again, what the fuck were you thinking?" Ms. Wauneta sharply screeched and glared angrily at Jean-Claude. Jean-Claude looked down and said quietly, "That is just it isn't it? I wasn't thinking and I was too scared I guess."

Monterey/Fort Ord

Jean-Claude arrived in San Francisco and Todd was at the airport waiting for him. It was 2300 and they piled into Todd's land barge of a car and drove to Ft. Ord; Jean-Claude was in California. Jean-Claude stayed at a hotel with Todd falling asleep next to each other cuddling. The next morning Todd took Jean-Claude to an apartment that he had found and Jean-Claude signed the papers that day, tossed his duffle bag inside and they headed to Ft. Ord so Jean-Claude could make arrangements to have his goods from Germany delivered to the new apartment.

Jean-Claude placed a call to Sam; he was dreading this call because he figured Sam would be very upset with him. With every right, Sam asked, "Why didn't you go to my sisters?" Jean-Claude didn't really have a good answer and gave some excuse; he could tell Sam was not happy. Sam raised his voice, "I came out to my entire family for you and expected you to go live with them. I made all the arrangements." Jean-Claude didn't have any answers for Sam and he knew that he had let Sam down, the guilt started to settle into Jean-Claude's body.

Jean-Claude found a job at a nearby law firm and settled into daily life in Monterey. Sam and Jean-Claude would write and talk to each other on the phone from time to time. Todd was spending the night over at the apartment a lot. Jean-Claude and Todd had sex one night after going out the club partying. Jean-Claude knew it was wrong and he would have to tell Sam. Jean-Claude kept putting off telling Sam because he didn't know how to handle the situation, Jean-Claude had done the thing he disliked the most, and he had betrayed Sam.

Sam called and didn't say hello but, "Who the hell is Todd?" "What are you talking about, he is a friend," Jean-Claude replied. Sam was upset, "I talked to your roommate and he told me everything." Jean-Claude was irate. Needless to say, the conversation ended in a fight and hurt feelings all around.

Jean-Claude waited for Todd to come back to the apartment that night. One thing with Jean-Claude was the longer he sat angry and thinking about it, the worse it was going to be for the other person. He kept playing the conversation with Sam over and over in his head. "Who does he think he is opening his mouth to Sam, which was my responsibility" He kept saying to himself. When Todd walked in the door, Jean-Claude unleashed which ended with Todd being kicked out of the apartment. Jean-Claude was done with Todd; he had been betrayed and could no longer trust Todd.

The following week, Jean-Claude received a letter from Sam. He was afraid to open the heavy envelope. He knew this had arrived too quickly and the last they spoke Sam was furious with him. Jean-Claude sat down on the floor and opened the letter to read the contents. Sam was done; he couldn't take any more of Jean-Claude's antics and broke it off with Jean-Claude. Jean-Claude lay on the floor in a ball crying for hours; he had lost the only person that truly loved him. Jean-Claude felt so horrible about what he had done to Sam and in his mind he went back to his childhood and referenced his biological mother and at that very moment vowed never, ever, cheat on anyone again. If things were not working out he would have to deal with the situation, but cheating was not acceptable under any circumstances.

> "Whoa, let me understand this…Sam tells you he loves you and wants to be with you, makes plans for you to stay with his family and you go in another direction running away from love. Then you cheat on him? Boy you certainly know how to make a big mess of things don't you?! Ms. Wauneta exclaimed. Jean-Claude knew better than to even attempt to defend his actions and sat quietly.

Jean-Claude buried himself in work trying to stay busy and not think of Sam because if he did he would just start to cry. He agreed to work any overtime that was available and would work himself to the point of exhaustion so he didn't have to deal with his feelings.

Several months later, Jean-Claude headed to a local gay bar. He was having a 'sex on the beach' at the bar when he heard the guy next to him say, "That doesn't give you a headache the next day?" Jean-Claude responded, "Don't know, first time I've tried it." They guy introduced himself as Bino and started a conversation with Jean-Claude. Bino was 5'7", 145 pounds, medium build Latino. After 30 minutes or so, Bino introduced Jean-Claude to his friends Dave and Hank. Dave laughed as he was introduced and Jean-Claude asked, "What's that all about?" Dave replied, "You have no idea what you have gotten yourself into." The guys danced and partied into the night.

Jean-Claude asked Bino if he wanted to go home with him and Bino quickly agreed. Bino went over to let Dave that he would not need a ride that night and he would be staying with Jean-Claude. Dave laughed and leaned over to Jean-Claude and said, "You are about to find out just how big Bino is, hope you can handle it." When Jean-Claude and Bino got home, naked and in bed, Dave was certainly right, Bino was at least 10" and very thick. The two started out with oral sex and then Bino said, "I can't get off this way, and I have to fuck." Jean-Claude wanting to make him happy agreed. It took some doing, but eventually Jean-Claude could accommodate Bino. When they were finished, Bino demanded that Jean-Claude drive him back to base. Jean-Claude agreed and off they went.

Over the next few weeks Bino ignored Jean-Claude and Dave started to hang out with Jean-Claude. Dave was a quiet, laid-back soldier from Texas who was 5'8", 155 pounds, black hair, brown eyes and a big package as well. One night when they were hanging out Dave grabbed Jean-Claude's crotch and they started to play around with each other. Jean-Claude was proven correct as he pulled down Dave's pants; he was large as well.

Over the next several months, Jean-Claude was part of a triangle physical relationship between Jean-Claude, Bino and Dave. One night, Dave asked Jean-Claude, "Who is that guy?" pointing across the room. Jean-Claude looked and said, "It is Todd." Todd saw Jean-Claude look and headed over to their location. Todd said hello and Jean-Claude introduced him to Dave. Jean-Claude figured Dave was interested in Todd and they would head off together, no big deal. Then Dave leaned over to Jean-Claude and asked, "Can we take him home to play with us tonight?" Jean-Claude replied, "Don't know you need to ask him?" Todd quickly agreed when asked.

> Ms. Wauneta playfully smacked Jean-Claude on the back of the head and said, "What a tangled web we weave Chickie. How does a smart guy like you get themselves into a mess like that? Thinking with the little head instead of the big head or were you just trying to replace love with sex?" Jean-Claude didn't respond because he knew she was right.

Jean-Claude needed to find a cheaper place to live than Monterey so Dave and he looked at a place in Salinas. They found a lesbian soldier and the three of them moved into a townhouse together. The boys took the downstairs rooms next to each other and the lesbian took the master bedroom upstairs. This was a good arrangement for all of them because they would go out to the field and wouldn't have to worry about anything. Jean-Claude and Dave were sleeping together regularly now but not entering a relationship. Jean-Claude didn't want anything to do with a relationship after what had just happened with Sam.

Moving Around

Jean-Claude took a week off from his job at the law firm and headed to San Jose for a few days. He found a gay club up there in Dameron's Guide called St. James and decided to go see what it was all about. Dameron's Guide was a lifesaver for gay men in those days. It was a book approximately two inches thick listing all the gay places in the US; they had them for locations all over the world. Jean-Claude had first found this book while in Germany.

St. James was a restaurant and bar/dance club in the heart of San Jose. Every night started out with a funny drag show and then the music started pumping. As you entered the swinging doors into the club, the bar was off to the left with seating along the bar and against the wall across from the bar. Through doors on either side of the bar was the large dance floor and stage area.

The resident drag queen took a liking to Jean-Claude during the preshow cocktail hour and invited him back to see the show. Jean-Claude figured why not, it was early anyway. As the drag queen got into her routine everyone was laughing and having a good time. Suddenly, the drag queen pointed at Jean-Claude and said, "Oh look at the fresh meat boys, he is so cute and tiny I could just take him home in my purse." Jean-Claude turned all colors of red in embarrassment.

Jean-Claude decided that he rather liked San Jose and decided to go see a headhunter the next day while on vacation. He had his appointment in the morning and that afternoon he received a call for an interview the next day. Jean-Claude went to the interview and landed the job. He was going to move to San Jose.

"Oh goodie, another drag queen in the picture, I like this more and more Chickie." Ms. Wauneta joyfully claimed. "And I like her too, because she gets boys like you out of their shell."

San Jose/Santa Cruz

Jean-Claude quickly found an apartment and moved in all in one weekend. His military life was paying off; he could efficiently move everything he owned in a very short period of time. Jean-Claude settled into life in San Jose and started to go to St. Jakes regularly.

Part of moving was making a call to his family and try to keep in touch in case his family would take him back. Jean-Claude placed a call and had another conversation with his stepmother. The normal information was given, new address and phone number and simple general inquiries on how everyone was doing. Hanging up the phone Jean-Claude was sad because he knew he would never receive a telephone call. This got him thinking about Sam again, if he had made the choice to move to New York instead of California, life would be different.

Jean-Claude decided to volunteer with the Gay/Lesbian Center in San Jose and he decided to deliver meals to those who had AIDS and were homebound. Soon Jean-Claude had a regular client list of five people and would deliver the evening meal each night after work. It was easy: arrive, knock on the door, deliver the meal and help get it prepared, see if the client needed anything and sometimes he and the client would discuss anything the client desired.

It was only three weeks into his volunteering that one of his clients passed away. Upon arriving to pick up the meals for the night the director of the program met him in the lobby. "Do you have a few moments for us to catch up on how things are going?" the director inquired. "Sure" Jean-Claude replied. They went to the director's office and he closed the door, "Have a seat. I wanted to see how things were going with the clients, but I need to let you know that we have lost one of your clients today.

You will not be delivering meals tonight so we can talk since this is your first client you have lost." Jean-Claude knew this would happen eventually and told the director, "No, I understood this might happen going into this assignment, everything is okay, I'm a little sad, but it is okay." The director looked at Jean-Claude assessing Jean-Claude's response and replied, "Okay, I just want to make sure. You also need to know that we have grief counselors on-site if you ever feel the need to talk about anything, just give them a call." "Okay" Jean-Claude replied and left for home.

Two days later, Jean-Claude was in the store staring at a rack of black suits when a clerk approached and said, "Can I help you with anything?" Jean-Claude just kept looking at the suits and shook his head no, quickly turned and left the store to his car. Once safely in his car he started to cry over the loss. After about two hours he reentered the store and approached the clerk, "Hi, I was in here before and I do need help getting a black suit to attend a funeral." The clerk smiled and said, "I understand, let's see if we can find you something and get you out of here." After paying for the suit the clerk said, "Come pick up your suit tomorrow afternoon it will be ready and come see us again should you need anything." Jean-Claude just stared at the clerk in disbelief thinking, "Someone has just died here and you are acting like nothing is wrong." As Jean-Claude was walking to his car he said in his head, "Cut the guy some slack, he didn't know Steve. Life does go on you know."

One of Jean-Claude's other clients was Ben, but Jean-Claude referred to him as "Booger-head" because it didn't matter what Jean-Claude did, Ben was just a pain in the ass. Jean-Claude had no idea how tall Ben was because Jean-Claude had never seen him stand up. Ben was always sitting in that big overstuffed chair of his with newspapers and books littered about all within an arm's reach. Jean-Claude didn't even know if Ben ever left this chair, but thought "at some point the bitch has to go to the bathroom." Ben had short salt and pepper hair, a thin face with what Jean-Claude thought at one time were brilliant vibrant blue eyes. The dark circles under Ben's eyes were a telltale sign that he was not sleeping much. Ben always wore the same pajama bottoms under his housecoat that looked like a throwback to the Gone with the Wind days of big plantations. The curtains, always drawn, allowing little light to enter. Through this whisper of light Jean-Claude could see the artwork and photos scattered all over the walls of the apartment and could not distinguish what they actually looked like. Once in a while Ben would have the reading lamp located behind the chair turned on.

Ben was not a shy person and could be extremely vocal about things. Ben didn't like this or Ben didn't like that and was always bitching about something whether it was about the food, current events or something that he saw on television. Jean-Claude took this for about four weeks. Finally, looking Ben dead in the eyes he said, "Look Booger-head, if you don't like it then get off your fucking ass and do it yourself since it seems no one can do anything right for you." Ben just broke out laughing so hard he started coughing. With tears streaming down his face, Ben took a breath of oxygen from his tank. With a sly grin and evil gleam in his eye he said to Jean-Claude, "Well, you lasted the longest of anyone that has been bringing this crap to me. Most are only trying to do a good deed to get rid of their past sins. I wondered how long it would take me to break you. Sit down honey." Ben was always Jean-Claude's last stop of the night because Ben consumed the most time. Jean-Claude pulled the ottoman near Ben's chair as Ben started, "You know, I like you, once you find your backbone you are an okay person." Ben bent over and pulled out a thin black book from teetering pile to the right of his chair. Handing the book over to Jean-Claude he said, "Take this book home with you, read it over and let me know if you can handle what I have written down. If you can't say so, but think hard about it before you agree to it since it will not be for the light of heart." Jean-Claude looked down at the worn cover of the book and said, "Okay, when do you want an answer?" Ben waived a frail hand at Jean-Claude and said, "When do you think, as soon as possible you ass."

Jean-Claude went home, made a cup of hot tea and sat down at the kitchen table and began reading the book Ben had given to him. The first page read, "The things I want to do before croaking." In typical Ben fashion, the book read exactly the way Ben bitched about everything. As Ben picked up the book reading as he approached the couch in the living room, a photo fell out of the book. Picking up the photo Jean-Claude saw a very beautiful woman in the photo. Wondering what relevance this photo had to the book, Jean-Claude quickly started turning the pages skimming for a reference to the photo. "Ah ha, there it is" Jean-Claude stabbed a finger at the book. Reading what was written caused Jean-Claude to break out into a roar of laughter: "Below is a photo which is to be given to the undertaker with explicit instructions: I am to be sent to my grave looking exactly like this without any changes." The book went on to list with precise detail the color of the eye shadow, length of the false eyelashes, color of rouge, type of lipstick and where a person would find the clothes. Jean-Claude had stumbled upon another drag queen.

The next evening while picking up the meals to be delivered, he stopped by the director's office and he continued to tell the director what had happened with Ben. The director smiled and said, "I thought something like this might happen with Ben. What do you plan to tell him?" Jean-Claude said, "Yes, of course." The director looking perplexed asked, "Why?" Jean-Claude simply replied, "Because he asked me to do this for him." "Well, in that case, we are going to pull your other clients away so you can focus on Ben if that is okay with you" he director stated. "Sure I guess" Jean-Claude shrugged.

Jean-Claude knocked and entered Ben's house using the hide-a-key as always and looked towards the living room at Ben, he appeared to be asleep in the chair. Jean-Claude quietly approached Ben thinking, "Oh God, please let him still be alive." Jean-Claude couldn't hear him breathing or see his chest moving so he slowly stuck his hand under Ben's nose to feel his breath. Just as he got his hand under Ben's nose Ben's eyes shot open. "What the hell are you doing? Look, this old queen isn't dead yet; now get your smelly hand away from me." Ben roared. Jean-Claude quickly yanked his hand away and mumbled, "It might be a good thing if we just put you down so you will stop tormenting people!" "I heard that you bitch" Ben stated, none too pleased.

Jean-Claude hurried off into the kitchen to warm up the meal and said, "Well you old hag, I decided to help you with your little book you gave to me. However, there are a few rules here if you want me to help. One, you will stop bitching at me about not liking the food I'm bringing over; I can't do anything about it. Two, once we start this little adventure, you are going to finish it no backing out on me. Three, every Saturday I'm taking you out of this house someplace. You have been here too long and I think if we ever got your ass out of that chair it would have a permanent ass print in it." Ben chuckled, "Good one ass. Agreed."

A few Saturdays later the weather had turned stifling hot; when Jean-Claude entered Ben's apartment, a rush of hot stale air hit his nostrils upon opening the door. Jean-Claude called out, "Ben, what the hell? Have you even gotten out of that chair? Open a window at least!" Ben looked defiantly at Jean-Claude and snapped, "If I could open a window, don't you think I would have done it by now?" It had never occurred to Jean-Claude that Ben didn't have the strength any longer to open his own windows. Jean-Claude went over to the window, threw open the curtains and opened the living room window. Turning to Ben Jean-Claude said, "Okay Mister, we are going out to the pool until this place cools down." Ben glared at Jean-Claude, "Are you fucking crazy? As soon as I hit the sun 'poof' up in smoke I will go. Honey this vampire has not seen the light of day for a long time, let alone been out in the sun!" Jean-Claude stood staring at

Ben knowing he was trying to get his way again, but this time Jean-Claude had a trick up his sleeve. Walking across the room where Jean-Claude had spotted a big floppy sun hat a woman would wear to the beach; he picked it up while turning to face Ben and said, "No problem, big floppy hat, check." Reaching into his bag and pulling out a tube of lotion, "Sun block, check." Reaching to the shelf Jean-Claude pulled off a light flowery scarf, "Scarf to cover up, check." Waiving the tube of lotion at Ben Jean-Claude said, "We have everything we need and you are going. Now get your ass out of the chair and we are going to the pool. I don't care what you wear either, can go naked for all I care, but you are going outside, you agreed remember?" Ben looked pissed but began the struggle of getting out of the chair.

Keeping an eye on Ben's progress, Jean-Claude went into the kitchen and started to make a pitcher of iced tea to take out to the pool with them. Ben slid to the edge of the chair, took a rest and started to mutter something Jean-Claude couldn't quite make out. Jean-Claude chuckled to himself and didn't offer to help Ben; he wanted Ben to do this himself. After about 20 minutes, Ben was standing in the doorway to the kitchen, "Okay bitch, you got me out of the chair when are we leaving?" Jean-Claude smiled and said, "Oh my, don't we look pretty?" Ben was wearing a white wrinkled long sleeve shirt over his pajama bottoms, his big floppy hat perched on his head with the scarf wrapped around his neck and draped flowingly over one shoulder. Ben glared and said, "Shut up bitch, you wanted me up, I'm up. Now let's go."

As they ventured slowly out to the pool area a few people were at the pool looking at the two approaching. As Jean-Claude opened the gate, two muscular good-looking jocks got up from sunbathing, each taking one of Ben's arms helping him to the only table with an umbrella. Jean-Claude put down the iced tea and pulled out the lotion and waiving it at Ben, "Okay, either you do this or I will." Ben waived a hand back at Jean-Claude, "you do it, don't care." Jean-Claude looked at the muscle boys, rolled his eyes with his head cocked towards Ben said to them, "Can you believe the attitude on this old bitch?" The muscle boys started laughing, "Oh we know, we live next door to her and visit a lot." Ben piped in, "Yeah, a lot of good they do me. Cute little beef cakes come over, torment me and leave me sitting in my chair all hot and bothered thinking of what I could have done to them in my prettier days. Jean-Claude this is Chuck and the other twerp is Darrell" Everyone cracked up laughing.

As Jean-Claude was slathering the sun block on Ben, he was listening to the conversation that followed between the muscle boys and Ben. Jean-Claude could tell they were actually pretty good friends. Ben told them that Jean-Claude was helping him with his book. Chuck raised his eyebrow looking at Jean-Claude and said, "Boy you are a glutton for punishment, he asked us and we said no because we love him too much."

The four of them settled in for a nice afternoon of conversation and iced tea. While Darrell was telling a story about Ben, Ben cut him off and looked at Jean-Claude saying, "Honey, I need you to start planning the park thing." Jean-Claude looked at Chuck and Darrell and could see the look of concern on their faces. Ben snapped, "Don't look at them for approval. They completely disagree with what I want to do, but trust me honey, they will be the first ones in line or I will come back and haunt them every time they want to have sex!"

That night Jean-Claude pulled out "the Book" as he began referring to it and looked up the park request. In it were detailed instructions to plan Ben's "Living Wake." Jean-Claude spent the next several weeks putting the plan together and had gotten Ben to pick a date for the event. With the help of Chuck and Darrell all the invitations were painstakingly handwritten to each invitee with the ever-present supervision of Ben. If a mistake was made Ben would snatch the paper out from the writer and throw it on the floor exclaiming, "Start again, that was a mess." It was amazing how many invitations were produced when Ben went to sleep in his chair.

Finally the big day came for the "Living Wake." Jean-Claude woke up early and drove over to Ben's house. When he arrived, Chuck and Darrell were packing up the trunk of their car. Jean-Claude waived as he walked by and Chuck said, "Be careful, she is in a mood this morning and is waiting for you." Jean-Claude rolled his eyes thinking, "Oh God, what now?" As he approached the house, Ben was standing at the door tapping his food and saying, "About fucking time you showed up ass. You need to get in here and help me now!" Jean-Claude glimpsed at his watch; he was an hour early, what could be so important. As Jean-Claude entered the apartment, he saw Ben gently pulling a wig out of a box. Ben turned to Jean-Claude while putting on the wig saying, "Honey, it is your lucky day, you are going to meet Miss Trixie today. Now give me that small box in the corner and open the front curtain, Trixie needs her light." Jean-Claude sat there watching Ben transforming into Trixie and smirked when she messed up the lip liner which got a good glare from Trixie in the mirror.

An hour and a half later, Trixie plucked, stuffed and taped in places you don't want to know was ready to head out. Jean-Claude said, "About friggin' time, we are now going to be late." "Oh, honey, you can't hurry perfection like this now can you?" Jean-Claude had to admit, she looked great.

> "Oh Chickie, I think you were a drag queen in another life...why else do you have so many fun and fabulous drag queens in your life? I really like this one, she is feisty!" Ms. Wauneta said as she sat down in front of Jean-Claude giving her complete attention to him.

Thankfully Chuck and Darrell had packed everything needed and had left a long time ago to make sure everything was set up and ready to go. All Jean-Claude had to worry about was getting the old queen to the party.

When they arrived at the San Francisco Golden Gate Park they were only 45 minutes late and an irritated Jean-Claude was parking. Trixie saw his irritation and said, "Calm down honey, this is my party and I'll be late if I want to be late, you have nothing to worry about, it will take care of itself." Truer words could not have been said as the entire day ran late.

One event that Ben had wanted, however jaded and ill-conceived it was to everyone else, was the "Urn Hunt." When Jean-Claude announced this portion of the afternoon he heard a gasp from the attendees and then someone shouted, "Leave it to the old hag to make us look for her dead body! How fitting, how many times have we spent looking for her ass because she was always late to every event she ever attended." The crowd roared in laughter.

On the way back to home, Trixie fell asleep in the passenger's seat. Jean-Claude looked at Ben with amusement; it had actually turned out to be an extremely fun event and Ben looked so happy all day. When they arrived at the apartment complex, Chuck and Darrell were waiting on the curb for them. Chuck smiled at Jean-Claude and said, "We figured you would need help getting the old gal into the house." With that they pulled Ben out of the car with little effort and carried him still sleeping into the apartment and deposited him in his chair.

Jean-Claude spent Sunday lazing around the house doing chores and getting ready to go back to work often thinking about San Francisco with Ben. Late in the evening the phone rang, it was Chuck, "Jean-Claude you need to come over, Ben is gone. They are coming to get his body, but you need to be here since you have the Power of Attorney." Jean-Claude rushed over to Ben's apartment in a fog. The next few weeks were filled with funeral arrangements, disposal of property as Ben asked as well as cleaning the apartment to be turned over. Chuck and Darrell

124

were great and helped out every chance they had as well. When one of them would run into a funny picture of Ben a story would follow often started with "remember this?"

With Ben's death, Jean-Claude just didn't have the heart to continue working with AIDS patients and spoke with the director of the Center. The director completely understood and said, "This happens a lot when a strong connection is made between a volunteer and client. We always encourage this bond because many of our clients don't have family in their lives and it makes things easier when they feel they can count on a single person."

> Ms. Wauneta dabbing at the corner of her eye quietly said, "See I told you I liked her. Why is it that you are so giving to drag queens and people around you, but when it comes to a relationship you have all these walls up?" Jean-Claude gazed at Ms. Wauneta and said, "Because with you and other people, they don't want anything from me, just me." Ms. Wauneta shook her head no and said, "No honey, remember what Annie Lennox said in that song, 'Everybody Wants Something.'" Jean-Claude knew the song very well and thought about it, Ms. Wauneta was right.

Jake

Jean-Claude had gotten to know Ms. Kitty, the lead drag queen at St. Jakes, and her lover, since he was there all the time. He didn't call them friends, just people he happen to run into. One night after Ms. Kitty finished her show, she came over to Jean-Claude and said, "There is a guy that wants to meet you honey, follow me."

That is how he met Jake. Jake was older, 5'10", 155 pounds, blond hair, blue eyes, worked out muscles, and was a musician. Jean-Claude took an instant interest in Jake because his chest reminded him of Sam.

Jake and Jean-Claude started to date but only saw each other once a week because Jake lived in Santa Cruz. Every Friday night Jean-Claude would drive from San Jose to Santa Cruz, spend the weekend and on Sunday drive back home to do laundry and get ready for the week. The more time he spent with Jake the more similarities between Jake and Sam started showing up, especially the way Jake held Jean-Claude it reminded him how Sam would hold him.

Eventually, Jake and Jean-Claude got into a relationship and moved into an apartment together. This was a very strange relationship for Jean-Claude. They both lived in the same apartment, but never slept in the same bed. Sex was few and far between if at all for months. It was as if everything changed the moment they moved in together. This continued for three years before Jean-Claude ended the relationship and moved to another apartment in the same complex.

Brad Reconnection

Jean-Claude had been living by himself for a couple of months and he got Brad's new phone number and gave him a call. Brad and Jean-Claude picked up where they left off as if no time had passed; this was truly a brother relationship.

Jean-Claude finally got the courage up and said, "I need to tell you something." Brad chuckled and replied, "What that you are gay, I've known all along." Jean-Claude fell silent. Brad continued, "It is okay, it doesn't make any difference to me at all, we are still brothers." Jean-Claude let out a huge sigh. Brad asked, "You were worried? No big deal dude. Except I have one question for you. That night you stayed over in my room when you were on the couch did you spend the night staring at me?" Jean-Claude quietly said, "Yes." Laughing Brad said, "I thought so, why do you think I went to bed in just my underwear and no blanket? I was trying to see if you would finally do something." Jean-Claude was in shock; Brad would have been okay if something had happened. Jean-Claude was so very happy that Brad was just accepting him for who he was without an agenda.

Jean-Claude decided to finally call his stepmother and let her know his address and new phone number. He hadn't spoken to his family since Germany, but felt it was worth a try to keep the lines of communication open in case his family decided they wanted a relationship with him. The phone was ringing in his ear and he heard his stepmother, "Hello." "Hi, this is Jean-Claude. I'm just calling to give you my address and phone number." he said. His stepmother replied, "Wait, I need a pencil…okay, go ahead." Jean-Claude gave her the information and said, "Well that's all I wanted to say, in case you guys needed anything." "Okay, bye," and his stepmother hung up.

Brad called a few weeks later and invited Jean-Claude to an air show he was doing in Southern California. Jean-Claude quickly agreed and plans were made to visit Brad. Jean-Claude took the Friday off work so he could make the nine hour drive to the Air Base in the middle of the desert. When he arrived he followed the directions to locate the plane, but he couldn't find Brad. Jean-Claude was standing with his back to the plane looking around when he heard, "Hey asshole what are you looking for?" Jean-Claude turned; it was Brad with a huge grin on his face. They greeted each other with a huge hug and Brad started showing Jean-Claude around the plane.

After the show was finished for the day, Brad and Jean-Claude went out for a quick dinner, stopping by the store along the way so Brad could get a bottle of Nyquil. Brad was staying in a bungalow on base so Jean-Claude was just staying with him. As they got ready for bed, Brad drank the entire bottle of Nyquil, Jean-Claude said surprised, "What the hell are you doing taking all of it?" Brad said, "Relax mother, I do it all the time, I'm getting a cold and they won't let me fly if I have a cold and I need the flight time." "Okay," Jean-Claude said as he grabbed a pillow off the bed and tossed it on the floor. Brad asked, "What do you think you are doing? You are going to sleep in the bed with me, there is more than enough room and I don't want to hear any arguments. If you open your mouth to argue I'm coming over there to hurt you." Jean-Claude knew Brad was serious and just climbed in bed.

Jean-Claude almost fell out of bed several times during the night because he was hugging the edge of the bed trying to stay as far from Brad as he could. All the while completely sexually aroused by the fact he was in bed with Brad. They woke up the next morning and Brad said, "You look like shit, didn't you sleep well?" Jean-Claude made an excuse about not being able to sleep in new places very well while thinking, "It is your entire fault ass, if you had let me sleep on the floor I would be okay."

Ms. Wauneta was laughing something fierce as she exclaimed, "I know exactly what that is like, it happened to me too pretty much the same way. You can't hug those few inches at the edge of the bed tight enough to keep away from something you really want."

To Jean-Claude's complete relief, during his visit with Brad the subject of him being gay never came up. Brad had treated him as if there was nothing different between them even though Brad had to know that Jean-Claude was attracted to him.

A couple of years passed, Brad and Jean-Claude kept in touch with each other occasionally. Jean-Claude picked up the phone one day and called Brad, "Hey, what are you doing the next week?" "Nothing," Brad replied. "Cool, do you mind if I come down to visit you in San Diego?" Jean-Claude asked. "Come on down."

Jean-Claude spent the week hanging out with Brad in San Diego and loved the city; so much so, he went back to San Jose and quit his job the following Monday. The following Friday, he was in San Diego. With San Diego being a military town with both the Navy and Marines, Jean-Claude felt right at home.

San Diego

Jean-Claude had driven from San Jose to San Diego at night and was exhausted when he arrived at Brad's apartment in the morning. Jean-Claude took a nap of a couple of hours, woke up, read the paper looking for an apartment. When he found the first one that sounded interesting he called and got an appointment to take a look at it. That afternoon, Jean-Claude was moving into the one bedroom furnished apartment. Next on the list was to get a job; Jean-Claude took his resume to a headhunter and secured a job starting the next day. Jean-Claude's job engulfed most of his time as he worked in the litigation department of a boutique law firm and there was always overtime to work. Brad had started a new job himself and they had lost contact again.

Jean-Claude missed Brad and he was still struggling with not being out at work and being out in the community. Jean-Claude made certain those two worlds never collided by making sure if he was going to any gay events and before getting close to the establishment he would make sure he didn't know anyone.

Jean-Claude would run every night after work to keep the stress levels in check. Every once in awhile, Jean-Claude would make the grueling trip up the hill from MCRD to Balboa Park; the same hill from the scene in Top Gun where Maverick is chasing Charlie on his motorcycle. However, Jean-Claude usually just ran in Balboa Park where he developed a conversational relationship with a male prostitute he would see every night at the end of his run. As Jean-Claude was cooling down after the run the two of them would have a cigarette and talk about any number of subjects. On Saturdays Jean-Claude would head to the park to play volleyball with a bunch of gay guys.

Jean-Claude lived just down the hill on Washington Street near the airport from the gay Mecca Hillcrest. Jean-Claude would head up the hill every Friday to a country western bar called Kickers.

Kickers was a small bar, but there was always something interesting happening; from line dancing and two-step lessons to dance competitions and drag shows. As you came in the front door and making a sharp turn to the right you entered and immediately ran into an oval-shaped bar. Off to the right was the electronic dartboard and to the left was the hardwood dance floor with a small stage at one end. He quickly made friends and played darts for hours when he was not out on the floor dancing.

On Saturdays, Jean-Claude would start out at Kickers and around 10:00 would head down to the bottom of Washington Street to a club in the industrial area called WCPC (West Coast Production Company). This was a massive warehouse dance bar with three floors. As you entered, paying a cover of course, there was a coat check area to the right and a couple of steps forward to the right was a long bar the entire length of the space. In the center was a large dance floor and on each end of the dance floor were two sets of large speakers with bars around the top of them. As you continue walking forward halfway down the dance floor there were stairs leading up to the observatory deck where you could stand looking over the dance floor. In the back corner of this floor was another set of stairs that took you up to the sundeck on the roof where you could talk with people without shouting over the blaring music.

The very first night Jean-Claude went to WCPC he met a much older gentleman who looked the spitting image of Colonel Sanders. Jean-Claude and he would spend time chatting before everyone starting arriving around 11:00. It was during one of these conversations that a manager from the bar joined the conversation and asked Jean-Claude, "Have you ever thought of dancing for money?" Jean-Claude looked at the manager strangely and said, "What do you mean?" "Dance on top of the speakers, we would pay you, we have seen you dance and like it." Jean-Claude looked at Colonel Sanders who was grinning from ear to ear who said, "Do it for tonight, if you don't like it you can stop." So Jean-Claude agreed.

> "Oh hey, this is where we met Chickie. I remember you up there dancing in your hat and boots without your shirt. I was so jealous of your body and you were so confident. But then when you were away from that box you were quiet as a church mouse. I've always found it very interesting how you flow between the two parts of yourself at times." Ms. Wauneta stated as she was packing a suitcase with costumes.

Jean-Claude had a couple of shots to get the courage to get up on the speaker, but up there he went. Jean-Claude was wearing black cowboy boots, tight jeans, a button up country western shirt and a black felt cowboy hat. As he was climbing up onto the speaker there were a few hoots from some of his Navy friends he had made and Jean-Claude quickly looked at Colonel Sanders for assurance. Colonel Sanders smiled and said, "Just do it, you will be great." Jean-Claude quickly lost himself in the music and started dancing. He was dancing so much he was getting hot and sweaty. He finally unbuttoned his shirt while he was dancing, but this only lasted about 30 minutes before he just took the shirt off. Jean-Claude was in good shape, he still only weighted 120 pounds, had a six-pack and could dance for hours from all the running he did.

Soon Jean-Claude was dancing at WCPC every Saturday making good money from tips and getting paid. Colonel Sanders was there every night and soon guys were giving Jean-Claude their phone numbers and wanting to chat and dance with him. Jean-Claude never danced with anyone at the bar since he was working and that could create problems. He would not drink with anyone at the bar either. However, he might mention to a guy that they could find him at Kickers on Fridays if they wanted to meet for a drink. Jean-Claude's cowboy image became the trademark while he was dancing, during the night the other dancer, who was a young slender guy as well would trade places from the back speaker to the front off and on through the night. Jean-Claude liked dancing on the speaker, he was in control and no one really bothered him for the most part.

Jake Reappears

One night when he was dancing at WCPC Jean-Claude felt someone grab his leg, turning and looking down he saw it was Jake. "Hi, what the heck are you doing here?" Jean-Claude said to Jake. Jake replied, "I live here now, are you working?" "Yes, give me a few and I'll be on break and we can chat. Wait for me over by the bar and I will find you." Jean-Claude replied. When it was time to take a break, Jean-Claude headed over to Jake where they had a drink and caught up on things. Jake gave Jean-Claude his number and said, "Give me a call tomorrow and we can go to lunch or something." Jean-Claude smiled and said, "Okay."

Jake and Jean-Claude hung out as friends for several months. Jake even took care of Jean-Claude after Jean-Claude had his wisdom teeth pulled out. However, things came to an abrupt end when Jake got involved with a young guy he had met. Jean-Claude and the boy did not like each other. Jean-Claude told Jake, "It would be best for all of us if I just don't come around because he keeps getting jealous and then you have a headache to deal with, it will just be easier." Jean-Claude never saw Jake and his new boyfriend again except for one time in Las Vegas in passing.

It was during this period that Jean-Claude decided to get his tattoos. The first tattoo was on his calf of Buggs Bunny and went smoothly with very little pain. Jean-Claude always liked

Buggs Bunny because he always won. The tattoo artist commented on the fact Jean-Claude's pain tolerance was quite high. Jean-Claude thought, "Yours would be too if you dealt with what I did growing up." The next tattoo was a different story; he got a tattoo of Buster Bunny from Tiny Toons on his lower abdomen. Placing it in such a way that when Jean-Claude wore jeans without a shirt it looked as if Buster was jumping out of his pants. Not sexual at all but he would certainly get comments when he was not wearing his shirt. This tattoo was so painful the tattoo artist tipped the chair back until Jean-Claude's back arched and his head pointing towards the floor.

Brent

One night at Kickers while he was waiting for his dance partner to arrive he saw a guy line dancing and Jean-Claude could not stop looking at him. The guy finally caught Jean-Claude looking at him and waved. Jean-Claude nodded and moved to the edge of the dance floor since his partner had arrived. After a couple of warm up dances, Jean-Claude returned to the side of the dance floor to join a few acquaintances that had arrived and he noticed the guy was standing there smiling at him. Jean-Claude said, "Hi." "Hi, I'm Brent." They spoke throughout the night when they were not dancing and ended going home together. Brent was 5'7", 140 pounds, muscled, large package and a very nice ass, with short brown hair and green eyes.

A few months into the relationship after Brent and Jean-Claude were living together, Brad had decided to stop by and visit with Jean-Claude out of the blue one day. Brent was still at work while Jean-Claude and Brad spent time catching up. Brent arrived home and Jean-Claude introduced him to Brad. Jean-Claude could instantly see that Brent was going to challenge Brad for some reason. Brad saw it as well and looked at Jean-Claude. Jean-Claude shrugged his shoulders in response to Brad and allowed the conversation between Brad and Brent to continue. As the conversation heated up, Brad suggested they settle the disagreement by wrestling. Immediately Jean-Claude told Brent, "You don't want to accept that challenge, he will put in into the ground and might hurt you. You don't know what you are getting yourself into." Jean-Claude looked at Brad and shook his head no, but Brad ignored Jean-Claude.

Soon the wrestling began and Jean-Claude just stood out of the way; he knew what was going to happen. As he had predicted, Brad pinned him to the floor and would not let up until Brent stopped in total submission. Of course, Brent ended up getting hurt physically as well has having a severely bruised ego. Brent was so mad he left the house slamming the door. Jean-Claude turned to Brad and said, "Okay, you know that was purely evil and you did that because you don't think he is good for me." Brad grinned and said, "You are correct. So when are you going to break up with that asshole?" Jean-Claude rolled his eyes and said, "Did I ever interfere with you when that one chick you were with not good for you?" Brad said, "Yes you did, you did it through my brother, I heard about that conversation! But you know you were right and you will admit I'm right at some point. I just don't like what he is doing to you." Jean-Claude look through Brad and said, "You have no idea what has been going on. I have not said a word to you about my relationship with him. You certainly have not been around to know anything about it, so stay out of it." Brad laughed, "See, if I can get you this upset with me over just suggesting I don't like him, I know I'm right."

Brent and Jean-Claude would spend almost two years together in complete turmoil all the time. Brent would leave often around 9:00 saying he was heading over to Kickers and would not come home until 8 or 9 in the morning which would lead to a knock down drag out fight. Jean-Claude knew this wasn't right, but he said to himself, "I have no proof of anything and who am I to demand anything." One night while at Kickers playing darts, Ted who was a friend of a friend walked over to Jean-Claude and said, "I need to talk with you. I know you don't want to hear this, but Brent is going to the Bath house down the street all the time. I know because I have seen him there." Jean-Claude said, "Okay" and turned to play darts.

Jean-Claude was livid but certainly didn't show it since Brent was standing right there. Around midnight, Brent told Jean-Claude, "I'm going to get something to eat." "Okay," Jean-Claude replied. As Brent left, Jean-Claude followed at a distance. Brent when to eat Chinese food and when he came out headed towards home. Jean-Claude continued to follow him. Brent stopped outside a white building look in both directions and headed inside. Jean-Claude didn't know whether to follow him in or just go home since he didn't know what was in this building, there was no sign or anything, but his guess was this was the bath house. That night Jean-Claude waited up for Brent and when he finally walked in the door around 5 in the morning, Jean-Claude launched in complete anger. The next few months were complete hell for Jean-Claude until they finally broke up and Brent moved out. Jean-Claude went into a tailspin, another relationship had blown up in his face.

> "Oh yes, I remember that little twerp. I didn't like him from the start, remember that? There was just something I couldn't quite put my finger on with him." Ms. Wauneta said while digging deep into the back of the closet.

Jean-Claude had to eat crow and tell Brad he was right after the break up with Brent. All Brad said was, "I know; just don't get yourself in that situation again." Jean-Claude felt like a two-year old being scolded for taking a cookie from the cookie jar.

Jean-Claude hid out at home for several months not going out to the bar, but keeping in contact with a few people. He was finding out that a lot of people knew what Brent was up to for a long time and they were talking about it behind Jean-Claude's back. Jean-Claude immediately thought about where he grew up and closed himself off. Jean-Claude decided he would severely guard information from that point on as it related to him.

Jean-Claude started thinking about Sam again for no particular reason other than to compare the relationships. They were very similar in the sense that Brent was Jean-Claude and Jean-Claude had become Sam. Now Jean-Claude knew how Sam must have felt when Jean-Claude cheated on him.

Brad Reappears

Jean-Claude arrived home after work and found a note on his door. The note was from Brad and it said, "Call me" with his phone number. Jean-Claude rushed into the house and grabbed the phone thinking something was wrong. Brad answered the phone; "What is wrong" Jean-Claude said. "Nothing, are you home?" "Yes" Jean-Claude replied. "Then meet me at the Marriott down by my house and we can watch the election returns." Jean-Claude agreed and they met at Marriott. Since Jean-Claude was a staunch Democrat and Brad was a staunch Republican it didn't take very long for a heated and passionate debate to ensue which would consume the entire evening.

Finally, Jean-Claude got frustrated because Brad kept insisting his guy was going to win and Jean-Claude knew, for a fact, differently. So Jean-Claude asked Brad, "You want to place a bet on it? And it has to be something significant." Brad looked at Jean-Claude with an evil smirk and said, "Sure, I'll put my ass on the line, if your guy wins you can have my ass sexually." Jean-Claude looked at him in shock, but not willing to relent accepted the bet. As the night grew longer Brad started to realize his guy was losing and Jean-Claude was chuckling and told Brad, "If you think I'm not going to collect what is mine you are very mistaken." Brad replied, "Then you have to collect tonight only."

As they were driving to Jean-Claude's house, Jean-Claude was hard as rock. All of his fantasies he had over the years of being with Brad were about to come true. Brad turned to Jean-Claude in the car and said, "Just so you know, I planned this. I've wanted to have sex with a guy and you are the only person I trust." Jean-Claude felt so special and honored and closer to his best friend. Jean-Claude and Brad had sex together and afterwards, Jean-Claude was riding on cloud nine. However, Brad couldn't leave fast enough. Brad would not speak to Jean-Claude for several months after that night. Jean-Claude felt so alone again.

When Jean-Claude recovered from his hurt of losing Brad and feeling it was his entire fault for allowing it to happen; he started to go out to Kickers again. There he met a drag queen named "Dolly" after the persona Dolly Pardon. She was one of the cigarette girls that walked from bar to bar in Hillcrest selling their wares. Jean-Claude became friends with Dolly and was enamored with the level of confidence she had with herself to go out in public in drag. Jean-Claude would never do something like this; it would be too much of a risk. Along the way he met "Edie" as well who was active in the community and got Jean-Claude to volunteer with the Gay and Lesbian Center in San Diego doing HIV/AIDS education.

> Ms. Wauneta was looking wistfully in the mirror and quietly said, "I miss those two girls. You know, they both gave up the drag? Yep, killed both Dolly and Edie off they did! The last I heard Dolly was in San Francisco and Edie is in Vegas."

One night Dolly called and asked Jean-Claude to join her for the night as her escort all he needed to wear was his western clothes complete with cowboy hat. Since Jean-Claude always wore it out to Kickers he didn't give it much thought and met Dolly at the designated time. Dolly walked in done up magnificently, the spitting image of Dolly Pardon. She came over to Jean-Claude and said, "Okay, we need to get going, my car is outside." "Okay, where are you taking me? Jean-Claude questioned. "Get in the car, I'll explain" as she walked outside. Jean-Claude followed, hopped in the passenger seat and noticed there were costumes in the backseat. Dolly got in, started the car and said as she pulled away from the curb, "We are going to a competition and I need an escort, it is a Dolly Pardon look-alike contest." Jean-Claude was thinking, "So far, so good." She continued, "You know that country western bar down by the mall? That is where we are going." Jean-Claude spun his head and exclaimed, "That is a straight bar. Are you fucking crazy, you're gonna get us killed!" Dolly laughed and said, "Where is your sense of adventure." Jean-Claude was thinking, "Typical fucking drag queens, they are out of control sometimes and now here I am involved, oh well maybe it will be interesting."

They arrived and entered the bar which was busy for it being only 8:00 p.m. a few people glancing in their direction as they walked down the ramp and over to the stage area to check in for the competition. Dolly looked at Jean-Claude with a sly smile and said, "Hon be a dear and get me a drinkypoo" in front of a bunch of couples there were milling about. Jean-Claude thought, "Oh shit, this is gonna be a long night and when she is finished, I will have to drive." Dolly was in rare form too, completely in character and was just having the time of her life. She grabbed Jean-Claude a couple of times and out on the dance floor they went for a "quick spin" as Dolly called it.

The competition was about to begin and Dolly grabbed Jean-Claude's arm and pulled him backstage to the dressing area. "You are coming with me and helping" while dashing on those ridiculously high heels. Jean-Claude turned the corner and there a bunch of women in different states of undress, he immediately looked down. Dolly caught this and shrilled to the other competitors, "Oh don't worry about my boyfriend here girls, he is queer as a three dollar bill tacked to a bull's ass." Everyone was cracking up and Jean-Claude settled into helping all the women change costumes the rest of the evening. While thinking in the back of his head, "if one of their boyfriends comes back to check on them, I'm toast."

The competition went well and it was time to announce the winners so Jean-Claude went out to the side of the stage. As they announced the winners Dolly's number was not called. Then they announced the overall winner – it was Dolly. Jean-Claude instantly thought, "Oh God we are in trouble because I know they are going to have him talk and he can't keep up that high-pitched voice for the duration and we are gonna be in a world of hurt." Sure enough, they interviewed Dolly and all of a sudden her voice cracked and then she said, "Yes, ladies and gentlemen, a drag queen has won" and pulled off her wig. Thankfully everyone thought it was great and they had a wonderful evening.

Jean-Claude was very comfortable around drag queens and found their friendship fun and unattached. He could relate to many things that they go through to become a woman and how confusing it can be while going through the process. One thing that amazed Jean-Claude was how Dolly was a different when they would hang out and he was a boy. Dolly was quiet, reserved and shy as a boy. Dolly explained, "When I throw the wig on, I'm a different person and I hide who I really am behind the makeup." Jean-Claude thought about this, he went through life hiding behind a facade all the time; he didn't need the makeup to do it though.

As part of Jean-Claude's normal day he would wake up, hop in the shower and begin the process of putting his "face on" to go out into the straight world. If he was around other gay men he was more relaxed, but kept the facade in place to keep from getting hurt or having someone really get to know him.

The Writer

Jean-Claude was hanging out at Kickers playing darts when he noticed the Writer. Jean-Claude's first reaction was, "What the fuck?" but put a smile on his face and said, "Hi, how have you been?" The Writer responded with a grin, "Good, I'm here working on a book and I finished the other one. You know you are in the book." Jean-Claude instantly didn't like where this was going but said, "Oh, good for you." "The book has a spot about you and Sam." The Writer said with a glint in his eye. That certainly got Jean-Claude's attention and he responded quickly, "Oh, well I will have to pick up a copy, where might I find one. I do think of Sam a lot." The Writer said, "Oh, I talk to him often I can put him in touch with you if you like. And I will give you a copy of the book. But I will warn you, it is not nice towards you as it describes how you dominated Sam." Jean-Claude glared at the Writer and exclaimed, "What, how, I'm not so certain that is what happened, but I will have to read it." The Writer looked pleased with himself and said, "Well I will give you a copy, but if you have something to say, you can write your own book."With that the conversation wound down and the Writer took his leave. Jean-Claude did not like this one bit and was nervous, "What had Sam told him? Why would I be in the book, it was supposed to be about Sam? Oh well, it can't be that bad."

A couple of nights later, the Writer showed up running into Kickers. "Hi, here is the book, I'm just running past and I will give Sam a call. Have a good night." Jean-Claude looked at the book sitting on the table. Jean-Claude opened the book and looked for Sam's name, found it and turned to the page and began reading. For the first time, Jean-Claude realized how Sam really felt; there it was in black and white. There was no fixing or controlling this mess.

Jean-Claude spent the next few days thinking about the book, what Sam had said and grew agitated. Jean-Claude was more upset over the fact that it was out there in a book and that

Sam had told the world something Jean-Claude considered private. Jean-Claude valued confidentiality and there were just things you didn't put out for public consumption. A relationship and what happens between two people is one of them.

The telephone was ringing, Jean-Claude picked up the receiver, "Hello?" "Hi, it's Sam." "Oh my God, hi, how are you doing?" Jean-Claude replied. "Good, did you read the book?" Sam asked. "Yes I did."Jean-Claude tepidly responded. "Well what did you think?" Jean-Claude took a breath and began the conversation of what happened with them. Jean-Claude could tell by Sam's tone that he was comfortable with what he had done and felt justified. Jean-Claude settled into this understanding and just accepted it and the two began talking about other things.

After his conversation with Sam, Jean-Claude closed down again and stayed away from people except to go to work. Jean-Claude was hurting all over again as the wounds were reopened. Sam and Jean-Claude broke off communication after that one phone call.

When Jean-Claude finally came out of his funk over Sam, he started acting out recklessly. He would frequent the bath house, go home with different guys from the bar, and hook-up with guys from a BBS board just to have sex. When he was having sex with someone he felt good about himself and the pain of Sam was slowly going away. He never stopped thinking of Sam, but the pain was subsiding.

> "Oh Chickie, how many times are you going to bang your head against that wall? Having sex just for the sake of having sex is just replacing a feeling that you need or desire for a short period of time. It doesn't solve the main issue." Ms. Wauneta said while rubbing Jean-Claude's shoulder.

Darren

During this period of recklessness Jean-Claude met Darren. Darren was 5'8", long black silky hair, a giant smile, green eyes, olive skin, very nice package and a very nice ass. Darren agreed to a hook-up and came over to Jean-Claude's house. It was suppose to be just a "hook-up" and nothing more, but after sex, they started talking. Darren was a student at a local university and didn't know anyone down here and this was his way of meeting people. Ding – warning sign; Jean-Claude didn't see it – they were both being reckless.

Jean-Claude and Darren started dating and saw each other almost every night. The relationship developed very quickly especially after Jean-Claude met Darren's parents under a family emergency circumstance. One day, Jean-Claude was at Darren's apartment when he saw some pills on the desk and looked at the name. "Hmm, never heard of those before," he thought, "Hey Darren, what are these for?" Jean-Claude inquired. "Darren explained that he was diagnosed bipolar and these helped. Jean-Claude thought, "Okay, no big deal," and never gave it another thought. Soon after Darren and Jean-Claude moved in together and carried on having a relationship together.

> "Oh yes, I remember Darren, he was the one with the beautiful long flowing auburn hair that all the drag queens wanted to snatch off his head. And those green eyes, they would just captivate you the way he looked at you." Ms. Wauneta said as she plopped down on the chair to try on shoes.

One time as Darren and Jean-Claude were sitting on the couch bantering back and forth and they started to wrestle on the couch. Darren accidentally hit Jean-Claude in the face hard. Jean-Claude immediately pushed Darren to the ground sitting on his chest glaring into his face he seethed, "Don't you ever fucking touch me like that again. If you are going to hit me, you better put me down and out because next time I swear to God I will take you out." Darren had a look of complete fear and replied, "It was an accident, I didn't mean it, I'm so sorry." Jean-Claude didn't hear him as he got up releasing Darren and putting on his shoes. Darren asked, "Where are you going?" Jean-Claude replied, "Out and away from you until my temper is under control. I'm afraid of what I might do to you at this very moment." Jean-Claude left and went to a nearby park to think about what had just happened.

Jean-Claude was a little scared because he could not recall exactly how he had ended on Darren's chest. All Jean-Claude could recall was the hit and the next thing he knew Darren was on the floor. Jean-Claude had never had this happen where he could not recall his actions. "What just happened and why did I react that way?" he asked himself. Jean-Claude knew he did not like being touched by strangers and would jump if someone bumped into him at the store on accident. Then Jean-Claude thought of being hit while he was growing up and how when he left he made a pack with himself to never allow another person to hit him. Jean-Claude was a little nervous because he saw just what could happen if he felt severely threatened.

A few months later, Darren decided to take a job with a very large company and they had asked if Darren could transfer to their Orange County store. Darren and Jean-Claude decided together this would be the best for his career and since Jean-Claude had a job that could transfer anywhere they might as well move. It was decided, they were moving to Orange County – Republican central.

Orange County

Darren and Jean-Claude lived in two separate apartments during the transition phase because they had signed a year lease on the San Diego apartment and Darren needed to move up to Orange County quickly. Jean-Claude would drive up every Friday night and back Sunday evening for five months.

During this time of separation, Darren was expressing some of his fantasies over the phone with Jean-Claude during their phone sex. Jean-Claude was a bit surprised, since he had a wild side as well, but had always kept it in check. Moving to Orange County was not going to help that side since Jean-Claude knew he would go back to hiding that he was gay; living two separate lives.

After both of them were together in Orange County and Jean-Claude had found a job they began looking to buy a home together. They found a nice townhouse and were moving into their first home.

Sex was getting extremely wild between Darren and Jean-Claude as both of them started living out fantasies they had held inside for such a long period of time. They would pull a slip of paper out of a bowl before heading upstairs and that would suggest that night's activities.

It was a normal life, for the most part, except Jean-Claude kept his two lives completely separate. This was easy since Darren and he wore wedding rings and everyone at work just assumed that he was married to a woman. Jean-Claude did absolutely nothing to dissuade these assumptions.

Darren came to Jean-Claude in the kitchen while Jean-Claude was cooking and said, "I want to get a piercing." Without looking up Jean-Claude replied, "Okay get one," thinking it was an earring. Darren said, "No, you need to stop and pay attention. I want to get a PA." "What's a PA?" Jean-Claude asked. Darren explained the PA (Prince Albert) piercing to him showing him on his penis how it would be pierced. When Darren finished he said, "I would like you to get one with me." Jean-Claude looked at Darren and saw how much he wanted this on his face and agreed.

Against Jean-Claude's better judgment and against all his reasoning he found himself on the table getting his penis pierced by a dominatrix. Darren had found this piercer and had extensive conversations with her to make sure everything was on the up and up and even checked out her references. Jean-Claude about jumped out of his skin when the needle went into his penis, it hurt like hell! After a week Darren's piercing healed up nicely, but Jean-Claude was having problems. After two weeks they went back to the dominatrix and she took a look and said, "Well there are a few people that are sensitive to a piercing is and can be irritable. What I recommend is take it out for a week and then put it back in; if it hurts again, you are one of the sensitive people." Jean-Claude followed the instructions and he was sensitive to the piercing so it stayed out.

The relationship took a turn when infidelity was discovered. Terminating the relationship immediately, dividing furniture, dogs assigned a home, bank accounts undone, everything was over. Darren and Jean-Claude had been together for seven years. Jean-Claude immediately went into a tailspin like anyone ending a relationship.

Jean-Claude went back to his reckless behavior and was hooking up with guys regularly over the Internet. However, this time he was getting bolder and living some of his fantasies. He started dabbling in the leather scene and found he was comfortable for the most part.

Leather Excursion

Jean-Claude found the leather community was accepting of people for whom they are and only applied certain personas for certain actions or relationships. Jean-Claude found a guy online that he befriended and they started having extensive conversations about Jean-Claude's fantasies and turning them into reality. Darren (not the same Darren) spent the time to explain the rules of safety, the classes that Jean-Claude could take to have a better understanding and then decide how he wanted to continue. Jean-Claude signed up for a few classes the leather community was having and Darren went with him. They were very educational and Jean-Claude found, for the most part, the "leather" side of things was mostly acting; you didn't have to live it 24/7. It reminded him of drama in school with a twist and you had to be comfortable with yourself enough to proceed.

Jean-Claude always had trust issues and this was going to be a big hurdle. For the most part, Jean-Claude was a bottom and as Darren put it, "That is perfect, no top can do anything to you that you do not allow and if they do it means a lot of trouble and headaches. Remember our community is small and people can talk." That made Jean-Claude nervous and he was not sure what to do about it. However, Jean-Claude being completely versatile began to think about his roles with the guys he had been with sexually. After careful examination he discovered that about 90% of the time he was the bottom in the encounter. He expressed to Darren and Darren advised, "You like to be in control and not give it up. That is okay, there is nothing wrong with that, it just makes you feel secure is all."

> Ms. Wauneta was sitting on the edge of her chair listening when she said, "Chickie, my, my, my; a dominatrix, leather daddies and boys…my we have been a busy boy. I didn't know this about you; there is a wild child hiding in there. I bet when the bedroom door closes the little freak in you comes out doesn't it." Jean-Claude chuckled and said, "A little bit."

Darren invited Jean-Claude to go to a leather event with him in Los Angeles. Jean-Claude agreed and Darren instructed Jean-Claude what to wear, "I want you in your tightest jeans, black work boots and a white t-shirt." Jean-Claude agreed knowing that Darren was putting him in the clothes of a "boy." As they pulled up to the location and parked, Jean-Claude noticed all these men in all different leather outfits, some rather innocuous and others very risqué.

146

The party was a "Tom of Finland" party being held in an old theater. As you entered a bar located to the front at the counter, bathrooms off to the right and left. As you went into the theater on the large stage were different demonstrations. There was a hallway on the far back left corner of the stage that lead downstairs to a dark room. If you wanted to smoke you had to go up the ramp and out a side door to smoke in the alley.

Darren and Jean-Claude were standing in a group of Darren's friends when a blond buff guy who looked about 21, 5'6" no shirt and all muscle walked by looking at Jean-Claude. Jean-Claude nodded and went back to the conversation with the group. Somehow the conversation turned to whether Jean-Claude was a "top or bottom." Darren was elusive and said, "He can be both really, it just depends on his mood. Tonight he is here as a boy, but that can change in an instant, trust me."

Jean-Claude left the group to have a cigarette outside where he met a few people and had a pleasant conversation. On his return to the group, Jean-Claude mentioned to Darren, "Gheesh, they have the heat really turned up in here don't they?" Darren grinned and said, "Then take off your shirt." Jean-Claude removed the t-shirt and tucked it into his belt. Several of the guys in the group were staring and a couple said, "Shit, didn't know you had all that under there!" Jean-Claude's six pack was out for display, his chest had developed nicely for a runner and the bulge in his pants was very prominent since Darren had him wear a cock ring. Jean-Claude turned red in embarrassment and one of the guys saw saying, "Don't be embarrassed; be proud of it." At that very moment, Jean-Claude caught the blond buff boy walking past and he turned his head to watch him walk by the group. Jean-Claude turned back to the group when he heard Darren say, "watch, the turn is coming." Jean-Claude looked at Darren and said, "What?" Darren replied, "Don't worry about it."

About five minutes later the blond buff boy walked by again, but was staring down at Jean-Claude's crotch. Jean-Claude snapped, "Hey boy, what the hell are you staring at, the bunny on my stomach or the bunny's carrot?" The boy turned red and started to stammer. Jean-Claude simply looked at him and said, "I'm still waiting for an answer." The boy very quietly said, "Both Sir." Jean-Claude said, "That is okay, my name is Jean-Claude and if you want I can introduce you to the group." At the same time he heard one of the guys in the group say, "Fuck Darren, you were right, he can turn on a dime. And look what he has chasing after him." Jean-Claude asked the boy his name and the boy replied, "Just call me your servant for the night, Sir." Darren pushed Jean-Claude and hissed, "Just go with it and leave it alone, you are the Master now." Jean-Claude instantly thought of what Sam had called him and how that made him feel, but he shook the feeling and stayed in character.

Jean-Claude received a telephone call from an old friend Bobby from San Diego one morning, "Hi, what are you doing later today?" "Nothing" Jean-Claude responded. "Good, we will be by your house around 3:00 to pick you up" Bobby said. Jean-Claude smiled, he knew he was in for an adventure. Bobby was a Navy Seal still in the military and his boyfriend Rob was a park ranger in San Diego. Bobby was 5'8", about 175, short military cut brown hair and blue eyes, all rock hard muscle. Rob was 5'9", short buzzed brown hair, green eyes and well muscled as well. Bobby and Rob were into the leather scene and their relationship was one of Master and Boy, Jean-Claude could not recount a single time Rob had refused a request from Bobby.

At precisely 3:00 there was a knock on the door. Jean-Claude opened the door and there stood Bobby and Rob. Bobby was decked out in leather from head to toe, including the leather cap. Bobby was wearing a red and black latex outfit that hugged his well-defined body revealing everything. Bobby entered first and Rob followed; Bobby looked at Jean-Claude in his jeans and white T-shirt and asked, "Are you ready?" "Yep, let's go on this adventure." Jean-Claude said as he was walking towards the door.

Jean-Claude always found it very interesting because when it was just the three of them Rob and Bobby would converse with Jean-Claude like any other friends, no restrictions. However, if there was someone around that was not considered part of the inner circle, Rob would go into his submissive role. Jean-Claude found this interesting because they slide in and out of these roles with ease. "Maybe because they had been together so long" Jean-Claude thought.

Bobby was driving as usual; he never allowed anyone else to drive when they went out. Jean-Claude liked to refer to this as Bobby's need for control. Jean-Claude didn't mind, it only meant he could relax and have a good time without worrying about driving. Jean-Claude was advised the three of them were going to Silver Lake, where Jean-Claude knew there were a few leather bars. Bobby was giving Jean-Claude the lecture; "you need to be prepared, it will be crowded and I know how you don't do so well in crowds. Also, you need to stick close to us because you will end getting yourself in trouble wearing what you are wearing." "Hey" Jean-Claude interrupted, "what is wrong with what I'm wearing, it is just jeans and a T-shirt." Bobby looked at Jean-Claude in the rearview mirror, "I know and people will get the impression you are a 'boy' and I know how you can turn your dominate personality on if you feel threatened. Just stay within eyesight of us. Also, if someone bothers you, please let me know and I will handle it." Jean-Claude looked at Bobby's head and snapped, "Yes, mom, I'm not a child and I can take care of myself." Bobby chuckled and replied, "I know and that is what I'm worried about." Rob chimed in, "Jean-Claude just do what he asks, it is easier and you know that."

They arrived in Silver Lake, parked and on the way to the bar they ran into a sex shop. Bobby looked at Rob with a very sadistically evil look and said, "Let's go inside here." Rob and

Jean-Claude followed. Once they entered, Bobby started to look at all the toys and quietly mumbled to no one in particular, "Hmm, nice. The things I could do with this." Jean-Claude looked over at Rob and Rob just looked back rolling his eyes and shrugging his shoulders.

After the little side trip to the sex shop it was time to go to the leather bar. It seems they were having a fund-raising event and it was packed. After they entered, Bobby showed Jean-Claude around the place since he knew Jean-Claude always needed to know the layout of a new place before he would be comfortable, Jean-Claude needed to know where all the exits were located. As they walked in the door they turned to the left and entered another room. Off to the right was a U-shaped bar without stools and to the right was a pool table where this massive muscle guy was playing pool and Jean-Claude took notice of the muscle guy. Going around the bar in the far corner was a shoe shine stand and past that were the rest rooms with a line waiting to enter the men's room. As they doubled back, past the entrance they headed out onto a patio where there was another U-shaped bar, a dartboard, a small stage was set up in the back and there were wall-to-wall men in all sorts of dress.

The three of them doubled back to the first bar and Bobby ordered three beers. Jean-Claude was talking to Rob about the muscle guy playing pool and Bobby said, "yes, I saw you looking at him. Go say hello if you want." Jean-Claude shook his head no since he didn't have the confidence to walk up to a stranger and start talking. With drinks in hand, the three went back out on the patio where Bobby started talking to anyone and everyone. There were so many people being introduced to Jean-Claude that he could no longer remember any names, just faces.

"Chickie what is it with you and your muscle boys? You always seem to attract guys that are in good shape. Ms. Wauneta questioned. Jean-

Claude shrugged, "Not sure, it just is I guess. I know why I'm attracted to them; they are like Sam, but I like guys a little out of shape too you know."

The three had finished their first beers and Jean-Claude volunteered to go back to the bar and buy the next round. Bobby said, "That is cool thanks, we will watch you so don't worry." Jean-Claude rolled his eyes at Bobby and said, "I'm a big boy and can take care of myself." Bobby replied, "I know and remember what I said in the car too." Jean-Claude spun and headed for the bar. On his way he got stuck in traffic and a guy headed in his direction was staring directly into Jean-Claude's eyes. Suddenly Jean-Claude felt a hand grab his crotch. Jean-Claude jumped and tried to back away, but the man had a firm hold on his crotch and squeezed even harder. Jean-Claude came to a complete stop staring at the guy facing him not showing any evidence he was in pain from the guy squeezing his nuts.

The guy just started back saying nothing. Jean-Claude's irritation meter started to hit the red zone. Jean-Claude glared at the guy and said, "What?" The guy just stared back saying nothing. Jean-Claude glared and hissed, "I said what? This is not the way to meet me if that was your intention, you will have to the count of three to remove your hand from my crotch or suffer the consequences. Do I make myself clear?" The guy just kept staring and clamped harder on Jean-Claude's nuts. Jean-Claude began to count, "One, two...three." On the count of three, Jean-Claude grabbed the man's hand that was squeezing his nuts and twisted quickly, flipping the wrist upward and applying his thumb to the palm and began pushing the hand towards the back of the wrist. Jean-Claude knew this would cause immense pain and stepped a little closer and said, "The pain will cease when you are on your knees in front of me and you apologize for grabbing my crotch." Jean-Claude applied more pressure and to let the guy know he meant business, Jean-Claude pushed extra hard causing severe pain. The guy dropped to his knees and Jean-Claude let up on the pressure a little. Jean-Claude felt someone grab his shoulder and he pushed the hand away. Bobby said, "Cool it, it is just me. What the hell did he do to you?" Jean-Claude quickly told Bobby what had happened. Bobby looked down at the guy and said, "If I were you buddy, I would do what he is asking of you or you will be there for some time and it will get extremely painful if I know him." With that Jean-Claude applied more pressure and the guy cried out in pain, "Okay, okay, I'm sorry." Jean-Claude immediately released his hand and took a step backwards as the guy got off his knees. Bobby smiled at the guy and said, "You might want to avoid him for the rest of the night. You thought you were going to pull a stunt on a 'boy' and you got more than you bargained for didn't you?" The guy didn't respond; just scurried off towards the patio.

"Damn it Jean-Claude, I told you to leave the animals alone!" Bobby said while laughing. Jean-Claude smiled back and turned towards the bar to get the drinks. When Jean-Claude returned to the patio with the beers Bobby introduced him to four guys they had been talking to while he was gone. One of the gentlemen said, "Nice work over there. That guy is always pulling crap like that on anyone he thinks he can get away with it." Jean-Claude looked towards the guy and said, "Well he just didn't know what he was getting into is all and I don't like being touched by people I don't know."

"Yes, I have noticed that about you. You always back away from strangers if you think they are going to hug you or put their arm around you. I've watched how artfully you can dodge the manhandling." Ms Wauneta smiled.

Since Jean-Claude was still being reckless he decided to have a group sex party at his house. He got online and put together a group of six guys to hang out and play together for the evening. One of the guys in the group was Adam who was a couple of years younger than Jean-Claude, 5"10, buff, shaved smooth chest, big arms, black hair and brown eyes with a great smile. Jean-Claude and Adam played and seem to only focus on each other while the group was playing around.

Adam

The next night, Jean-Claude received a telephone call from Adam asking him out on a date. "When would you like to go?" Jean-Claude asked. "How about tonight?" Adam asked. Jean-Claude agreed and hopped in the shower to get ready since he had just returned from his run. Adam came by and picked him up and they went to dinner and a movie. After the movie Jean-Claude invited Adam to spend the night, as he agreed they started kissing.

Adam and Jean-Claude began dating seriously and a few months later, Adam moved into Jean-Claude's house. Jean-Claude was selling the townhouse and buying another house. Between work and two escrow accounts things were busy for Jean-Claude and he didn't see Adam too much during those 60 days.

After Adam and Jean-Claude had moved into the new house and had unpacked most of their stuff, Adam's friends that liked to go up to West Hollywood demanded to take them out for a little fun. Adam and Jean-Claude were the only couple; the rest were all single. It was interesting for Jean-Claude to be around a bunch of single people when in a relationship.

The friends took them to a dance club that played great music and the dancing kept going for hours, it was also known for drugs or people on drugs that were there. Jean-Claude had left his drink with Adam and the group and after he returned and finished his cocktail, about 30 minutes he didn't feel so well. Jean-Claude told Adam what he wasn't feeling well. Adam got one of his friends off the dance floor and told him what was happening. Adam's friend looked at Jean-Claude and said, "Yeah, I put an ecstasy tablet in your drink so you would relax and just have fun." Jean-Claude was furious; he had never done any drugs and now this! Jean-Claude demanded they go home immediately and walked off, since he had the keys he knew he could drive away and in Jean-Claude's mind, if Adam did not follow, he could find his own way home. Adam did follow and Adam drove them home.

A couple of days after the incident Jean-Claude told Adam under no certain terms that he never wanted to see that friend again, didn't want to talk with him and certainly never wanted to see him in the house.

Jean-Claude had been looking for a job during the sale and purchase of his homes as well. He went to an interview and learned about a new and exciting opportunity. Jean-Claude went back home and had an extensive conversation with Adam about this opportunity. Jean-Claude outlined the job, the salary, his career goals and what this job would actually entail. One of the major disadvantages was that Jean-Claude would be working very long hours since the company was building a new division and offering new products to its client base. Adam agreed this was a good opportunity and understood the constraints that would be placed on the relationship because of the job.

Jean-Claude started the new job shortly afterwards and everything was pretty good, he was only working eight to ten hour days six days a week. About four months into the new job, major changes were made in the department and two large clients were brought on board. Jean-Claude started going into the office at 3:00 a.m. and would not return home until 11:00 p.m. six days a week. Every other week, for a few months, Adam would go to the office and have dinner with Jean-Claude.

Adam and Jean-Claude had made plans before he started his new job to spend a week in San Francisco to exchange vows and rings. Since Adam was planning the entire trip himself, Jean-Claude asked if they could cut the trip down to just three days since work was eating so much of his time. Adam wasn't too happy about the request, but agreed to cut the trip short. Adam and Jean-Claude left on a Friday late morning and they were back by Sunday afternoon. As soon as they returned, Jean-Claude started working from home checking emails.

Jean-Claude thought he would be able to start reducing his hours when he was told they would be adding two more large clients his boss would be resigning from his position. Jean-Claude was promoted to Assistant Vice President, received a large bonus and the ridicules hours continued. Not only was Jean-Claude spending a lot of time at the office, but he spent a lot of time at home working as well. Because it was company policy that all AVPs and above were on call 24/7 Jean-Claude would go to bed with the cell phone on the nightstand and his laptop right next to it.

The first real fight came after Jean-Claude received a telephone call at 2:30 a.m. on his cell phone and he logged onto his computer and proceeded to have a three-hour conference call in bed with the east coast. When Adam expressed his frustration, all Jean-Claude could say was, "You knew this going in and you agreed so what do you want me to do about it?" Adam backed down and the argument ended.

The arguments would come roaring back when Adam would wait up for Jean-Claude to get home just to talk to him – all Jean-Claude wanted to do was go to sleep. Jean-Claude became irritated over this scene because Adam would start just as Jean-Claude was walking in the door. No matter how many times Jean-Claude asked to have at least 15 minutes to decompress from work and then start talking Adam would ignore the request. Jean-Claude started building up resentment.

Jean-Claude's birthday was coming up and Adam asked what he wanted for his birthday and Jean-Claude said, "Just sleep." Adam replied, "No, I'm serious, what would you like, anything just ask." Jean-Claude just smiled and said, "That is really sweet, but no nothing, I'm fine." Jean-Claude was still doing the same thing he did when he was a child – if you ask for nothing they have nothing to hold over you or take it away and hurt you.

Adam decided to throw a surprise birthday party for Jean-Claude. Jean-Claude did not like surprises at all. Adam woke Jean-Claude up early in the morning of his birthday which happened to be a Saturday and rushed him out the door to go to the coffee shop to relax. Jean-Claude whined all the way, but once he had coffee mellowed out. When Adam asked to go to the mall afterwards Jean-Claude shot him a look like "really, do we have to go?" Adam convinced Jean-Claude to go and off to the mall they went.

Two hours later they finally returned home. Adam went in the house first and Jean-Claude was pulling the bags out of the car while the dogs were jumping in and out of the car sniffing the bags for goodies for them. When Jean-Claude entered the house he dropped the bags when he heard, "Surprise, Happy Birthday!" Jean-Claude didn't say a word, he shot a sharp glare at Adam bent over picking up the bags while saying, "Oh, well thanks, I'm surprised I had no idea." Jean-Claude was fuming, not only because it scared the hell out of him, but also because these people were in the house when they were not home. Jean-Claude felt violated. Another reason Jean-Claude was getting very irate was because the guy who slipped the ecstasy into his drink was there, in direct violation of what Jean-Claude had told Adam.

The party was short, it only lasted two hours and when the final guest had left and the door shut, Jean-Claude turned to Adam and said, "You and I are going to have a conversation right now." The argument was a heated conversation, but ended with setting boundaries.

Newly promoted to Vice President, a Supervisor in Jean-Claude's department said, "Congratulations, but if we have to look like you and work like you to get promoted, count me out." Jean-Claude turned around and looked at the other two individuals who had been promoted at the same time and all three of them looked like the living dead: eyes puffy, red, bags under them, faces pale and exhausted.

Jean-Claude kept up the six days a week schedule for another two years. Adam and he were talking less and less and when Jean-Claude had free time Adam had made other plans. Jean-Claude really didn't worry about things too much, since he was working so much, Adam needed to have a life too. So he wasn't around, no big deal, Jean-Claude just slept and hung out with the dogs at the bark park anyway.

Several months later, Adam was going to an all-day conference for his work on a Saturday. It just so happened Jean-Claude was home from work for the entire weekend because the network was physically being moved and no one could work that weekend. While Adam was gone Jean-Claude decided to take the dogs go to the office and see how the move was going on the way to bark park. Jean-Claude was gone about an hour when he realized he left the cell phone at the house. "Oh well, work won't bother me because no work can be accomplished anyway, and Adam is at his conference and will be busy, no need to go home and get it." When Jean-Claude returned several hours later Adam's car was in the driveway. Jean-Claude entered the house and said, "What are you doing home so early? I thought it was going until late tonight?" Adam looked angry and said, "It is, but I called you several times and you never answered or returned my text messages." Jean-Claude reached over to the kitchen counter and picked up his cell phone and held it in the air, "I forgot the cell phone and I just got in the door."

Adam began asking Jean-Claude where he was and when Jean-Claude answered Adam began accusing him of lying. Jean-Claude was getting so angry he picked up the cell phone and called the guys at the office. As he handed the phone to Adam he said, "Ask them, I dare you, fucking ask them if I was at the office and when I left the office." Adam spoke into the telephone asking when Jean-Claude had gotten to the office and when he left. When Adam got off the phone, Jean-Claude said, "Satisfied?" Adam stated punching buttons on Jean-Claude's cell phone and Jean-Claude watched as he began going through Jean-Claude's email, text messages and phone logs. When Adam looked up he said, "I know you have been cheating and you probably just erased everything so I wouldn't find it."

Jean-Claude reached out and pulled the cell phone away from Adam while saying very quietly and glaring at him, "You just crossed the line, give me my telephone. I will leave and I will return in three hours, I would suggest you be here when I return. Do not call me as I will not answer the telephone." Jean-Claude left and headed over to a local straight bar where he ordered a beer and proceeded to watch television. Jean-Claude's telephone rang 15 minutes after he got to the bar, he looked down and saw it was Sarah, a good friend of his, calling. Jean-Claude answered the phone and his friend said, "Where are you?" Jean-Claude replied, "At your bar, why?" "I'm headed over there right now, stay put" she said. Jean-Claude thought, "Strange, but okay."

A few minutes later Sarah arrived since her office was just down the street. They said hi to each other and Sarah got her beer and asked Jean-Claude, "So what has been going on?" Jean-Claude replied, "Not much just wanted to get out of the house for a drink." Sarah smacked him on the arm, "You ass, I talked to your other half. He told me what happened. I asked him if you were very quiet before you left the house and he told me you were. I told him that you were very angry and it wouldn't surprise me if you came home and cut his nuts off." Jean-Claude chuckled, "He is close, very close, and little does he know." Sarah looked at Jean-Claude and said, "He's gone isn't he? There is no way to fix this thing is there?" Jean-Claude looked at Sarah and said, "Nope, he crossed the final line by accusing me of cheating, you know what happened to me when I cheated on someone... so does he damn it! Monogamy was a condition of us even being together." Sarah asked, "Do you want to know what I think?" Jean-Claude replied, "No, I already know, if they accuse you of cheating they most likely doing it themselves." Sarah simply nodded and said, "Well I'm here if you want to talk, but I know you it goes very dark before you start talking."

Jean-Claude returned home and walked into the living room where Adam was sitting crying. Jean-Claude said in a normal calm voice, "Here is what I have to say and listen closely since I will not repeat anything. How dare you accuse me of cheating, the only reason you would ever think of accusing me of that is mostly because you are cheating. Trust me, it will come out that I'm correct. Further, this relationship is now over effective immediately. I will give you one week to get out of my house and within three weeks we will have everything settled between us with regard to bank accounts, etc. Since I'm the only one listed on the house and it was my money that purchased the house, do not even attempt to go after it. I am finished with what I have to say and I will not discuss this further period so don't even try. I will move into the guestroom."

In his mind, Jean-Claude had a list of items which he considered violations. If any of those lines were crossed and he felt a person had done him wrong, he would cut them off without a second thought. He might run into them in a social event and it would be extremely unusual even for him to say hello. Jean-Claude's thought process was that if a person did it once they would do it again and could never be trusted.

Two days after Adam moved out, it was Jean-Claude's birthday. Jean-Claude was alone with the dogs in the house and he began to perform an autopsy on his failed seven year relationship with Adam. It was during this examination that Jean-Claude cried for the first time since his last conversation with Adam where he had ended the relationship.

Jean-Claude didn't go out after his relationship ended, just stayed home and went to work. After three months he went to see Human Resources at work where he had become good friends with Barb the VP of HR. When he came into the office he said, "I need about 30 minutes of your time and we need to pull my file." Barb said, "Oh no, what happened?" Jean-Claude simply stated, "I need to remove Adam from all my paperwork." Barb looked at him in shock, "I had no idea you were going through a break up, you certainly never showed it." Jean-Claude chuckled, "Yes, if I don't want people to know something, they will never know."

Several months later, it was Pride season and Jean-Claude decided he would go down to the San Diego Pride; it had been a long time since he had been there, and he probably wouldn't run into anyone that he knew. Wrong, Adam was there and as chance would have it was in a situation where Jean-Claude couldn't get away. Adam said, "Hello." Jean-Claude stared coldly and said, "Hello." Adam introduced Gary the guy he was with and Jean-Claude said, "It seems I know you from someplace." Gary replied, "No, I've never met you." Jean-Claude glanced at Adam quickly and Adam would not make eye contact. Jean-Claude's attention focused like a dog with a fresh bone, "there is something here, now to figure out what it is" he thought. Jean-Claude turned to Gary and said, "So what is it you do for work?" Gary said he was a broker and Jean-Claude inquired where his office was since he knew people that worked for the same company as they were one of Jean-Claude's clients. Then it quickly dawned on Jean-Claude, "I know you now. You are a manager for the distressed property side of your company. You and Adam have met to discuss working with his company. Didn't you meet about four or five years ago?" Gary said, "Wow, you have a good memory, yes about five years ago." Jean-Claude had figured it out and went for the kill, "It is strange that you both have remained such good friends after all this time to come here to Pride when the business deal fell apart. Unless, of course, and I will make the presumption that I will be right with this next part, you were fucking around with each other behind my back." Dead silence from Gary, Adam and anyone nearby. Jean-Claude flashed an angry look at Adam and exclaimed, "I told you I

160

would find out and that I would be proven correct. You disgust me, five fucking years of the seven we were together? If you were that unhappy why didn't you feel around for a pair of balls between your legs and get out of the relationship? Whatever, dude just go away and if you ever see me, head in the other direction."

Jean-Claude returned home and the long healing process began. Jean-Claude didn't go out for five years but that was also partly due to what was next to come. Jean-Claude decided to go and make sure Adam had not infected him with anything so he made an appointment for all the testing. A week later, on the Wednesday before Thanksgiving, Jean-Claude returned to the doctor's office and was advised that he was HIV positive.

Jean-Claude sat in the chair just staring at the floor; he couldn't believe what he was hearing. The counselor asked, "Are you okay? We can spend as much time as you need if you want to talk." Jean-Claude shook his head no and asked, "What is the next step?" His mind was racing and he could not keep track of all the thoughts that were all attempting to be processed at the same moment. After making an appointment to come back in two weeks Jean-Claude headed home.

When he went into the house he was texting a friend he had made plans with saying, "Not feeling well, going to cancel our plans this weekend." Jean-Claude hit send, turned off his cell phone and tossed it on the kitchen counter. He plopped down in front of the television, aimlessly began flipping channels until one of the dogs pushed on his hand. When he looked at the little face looking back up with the wrinkled forehead Jean-Claude just started crying. Jean-Claude spent the entire four-day weekend thinking and crying.

The typical thoughts entered Jean-Claude's mind of course. "Why me? What am I going to do now? No one will ever want to be with me. Oh well, it will just be easier to be alone anyway." To the cynical thoughts, "Well I guess that settles it then, I can never go back home." As he recalled the conversation after telling his stepmother he was gay. "Like it really matters, my family has never tried to contact me anyway." Or the "All the one night stands I've had and reckless behavior and never caught a single thing, but I get this from a crappy-ass relationship, go figure."

Jean-Claude went into a tailspin for several months after this discovery. At work he was fine, but when he got home he would enter a completely depressed state. He even went so far as to get rid of any goals he had since those wouldn't matter any longer. He began thinking off all the people he had lost in life to this disease and what they had went through, he was scared.

> Ms. Wauneta put his arm around Jean-Claude and said, "I remember that time too. Remember you never told me, I just guessed. But we got caught up on all the movies we had wanted to see over the years and ate lots of ice cream didn't we?" Jean-Claude smiled and nodded in agreement.

Jean-Claude worked with the doctors on a treatment plan for him he began to gain control over the physical aspects of living with HIV. Jean-Claude knew enough about HIV/AIDS, but now it directly affected him and he now needed to deal with the side effects of the medications for six months until they settled down and went away. Jean-Claude was lucky in the strain of HIV he had contracted was very weak and not drug resistant to any medications.

Jean-Claude dealt with his emotions of having HIV by himself; like he did everything else in his life, don't tell anyone and keep it a secret. He never told any of his friends and he stopped having sexual contact with anyone. He would go hang out in a local gay bar in Orange County, which was one of a handful. He made a few friends there, but never could feel close enough to any of them to discuss his HIV status.

One afternoon he ran into older gentlemen, who happen to sit next to him at the bar. The struck up a conversation and they guy introduced himself, "Just call me Grandmother. You can tell me anything, I don't talk to anyone." Jean-Claude chuckled to himself and proceeded to have a wonderfully intellectual conversation since most conversation in a bar is mundane and boring to Jean-Claude's standards. Jean-Claude's relationship with Grandmother grew into a bar relationship only and Grandmother would suggest books for Jean-Claude to read. As Jean-Claude would work through these books he discovered that Grandmother knew much more than he was letting on to anyone. Jean-Claude never told Grandmother about being HIV positive and lost contact with him when he moved to Long Beach.

Jean-Claude found a job working for a large Orange County company which was extremely conservative. Jean-Claude went fully into the closet until one day the office was having a conversation about a ballot initiative to outlaw gay marriage in California. Jean-Claude always being politically involved took part in the conversation. At one point a female co-worker said, "I don't want my kids taught about gay marriage in school." Jean-Claude laughed and said, "It has nothing to do with what taught in school. Furthermore, if you are so concerned with what your kids are taught, get involved with the PTA or get elected to the school board. The more important point is the fact that heterosexuals who get married have more than 1,000 rights given to them that are denied to gays and lesbians even if they get a Domestic Partnership in the State of California. A better solution would be to outlaw divorce or better yet, outlaw marriage all together. You cannot say 'Yes, let's have marriage, but yet deny a group to the right of marriage.' Marriage is between you, your partner, your God and your church; the State has no right to get involved in marriage. Additionally, it violates not the State Constitution of equal rights. This initiative takes a group of individuals, specifically identifies them and then discriminates against them. The ultimate question is this: 'If they are allowed to get married, how does it affect you in any manner?' The answer to that question is: 'They don't affect you.'" The co-worker asked, "Why is this so important to you?" Jean-Claude took a breath and quietly said, "Because I'm gay and it affects me directly you are going to discriminate against me and if I ever want to get married I can't. You are effectively saying I'm nothing, I have no rights, I'm a second class citizen, I didn't not spend time in the Army to defend the rights of others to discriminate against me. The majority of people cannot tell a minority of people they have no rights." Jean-Claude was shaking nervously to see how his co-workers would react to his coming out as gay. To his surprise, the female co-worker said, "I will vote against the proposition. You are the first gay person I've personally known and you make a point.

For Jean-Claude it felt good to come out at work, his personal life had collided with his professional work after all these years and nothing horrible happened. It had taken a very personal political issue to ignite his passion to a point that he did not care who knew he was gay. However, this period of being completely out and open would not last long.

Long Beach

Jean-Claude decided to move up to Long Beach and get away from Orange County. First it was because he spent a lot of time up in Long Beach where it was more "gay friendly" and had many more things to do for gay men. The other reason was that he was tired of living in a county that was dominated by republicans, no offense; he just didn't have a lot in common with them. However, Jean-Claude returned to the closet to hide who he really was again.

Jean-Claude started to go out meeting people at the bars, but no one he was interested in for anything other than a conversation in a bar. Jean-Claude always thought it was funny how people would introduce each other at a bar as "my friend" when; in fact, they were nothing more than bar acquaintances. Jean-Claude got hit on by a few guys during this period and just made it difficult for them to even go on a date. Jean-Claude would employ the old excuses of "I work a lot." "I'm really busy right now and don't have time to seriously date anyone." "I'm not looking to date anyone right now." Jean-Claude was perfectly fine being single and by himself. A few guys who hit on him might reply, "I'm not looking to date long-term either, I just want sex for the night." Jean-Claude referred to these guys as part of the "Catch and Release Program." Go home, have sex, go your separate ways, no phone numbers exchanged and if you ran into each other in the bar it was a nod of acknowledgment but nothing more.

Jean-Claude did engage in the "Catch and Release Program" a few times and was surprised how many people would be willing to go to bed with someone without asking about HIV status. If Jean-Claude wanted he could have kept his mouth shut, but he had a responsibility not only to himself but to his sexual partner to disclose. So long as they were part of the Catch and Release Program, Jean-Claude could tell them in passing and if they still wanted to go home, then he would take them home. No questions asked.

However, he met a few guys that he had gotten to know and that he liked for just more than a quick hook-up. These guys, he always found a way to end it before it really had a chance to develop into anything resembling dating because he couldn't find a way to tell them that he was HIV positive. The one time that he did mention he was HIV positive to a guy he was interested in the guy stopped talking to him immediately.

Jean-Claude did find a guy that he started dating for several months where he had told him that he was HIV positive and the relationship continued to develop. However, after several months of investing time, Jean-Claude started to wonder when they would become sexually involved and started pushing in that direction. As they started having sex, the guy said, "I'm sorry I just can't." Jean-Claude understood what was being said and let the guy leave never speaking with him again. After that experience, Jean-Claude went back into the closet and closed himself off from everyone.

Jean-Claude ended staying in a community of Veterans. If you didn't know specifically where the property was located, you would have no idea it existed. It was the perfect place for Jean-Claude to hide and he started to relax a bit, it was like coming back home, he was surrounded by people that he had something in common with and who might understand him. Jean-Claude had entered a slow crash and burn without realizing it was happening. He was going through life on auto pilot without any specific goals or ambitions in life.

Jean-Claude volunteered to help out at a nonprofit event with a bunch of Veterans at the Long Beach Gay Pride. They had a great weekend and several people were surprised to see a group of Veterans actively seeking gays and lesbians to join and get information out at a Pride event. This was an interesting position since every volunteer was a gay or lesbian Veteran.

Jean-Claude met Ge a 6'1", dark hair, brown eyes, 190 pound buff Chinese man who was living in Long Beach with his sister just down the road from where Jean-Claude lived. Jean-Claude was immediately very physically attracted to Ge as he reminded him of Sam in the way he looked and carried himself. Ge had the same self-assurance that Sam had and Jean-Claude enjoyed being around. Ge asked Jean-Claude out on a date and when they were walking along the busy city street in downtown Long Beach after dinner, Ge put his arm around Jean-Claude, leaned down and kiss Jean-Claude in front of everyone. At first, Jean-Claude stiffened and thought of all the people that might be looking and Ge pulled him in even tighter, Jean-Claude let go of his fear and kissed back. Jean-Claude was happy, he felt safe for the first time in a long time. Surprisingly after telling Ge he was HIV positive at dinner, Ge seemed to be okay. They began having sex that night.

Jean-Claude was seeing Ge every chance he could. Things were progressing well until one night, after four weeks of dating, while walking on the beach, Jean-Claude turned to Ge and said, "If it would okay with you, I'd like to seriously date you and work toward a relationship." Ge paused and said, "Well that would be nice and wish I had met you a year ago. I'm not a very good guy and I think you believe I'm a good guy. But I have a boyfriend in China." Jean-Claude fell silent, hurt. Jean-Claude immediately pulled his hand out of Ge's hand and looked down. He was disappointed and thought, "What the hell? How did I miss this? I know I didn't specifically ask, but damn!" Ge asked quietly, "Are you mad?" Jean-Claude replied, "No, just disappointed because I had hoped for more, but I guess it cannot be, I'm sorry." Ge said, "I'm sorry, but I needed to be honest with you before you got your hopes up." "Well, that is a little late. You should have said something earlier. It is okay, but I cannot continue having sex with you because that's cheating and I've been on both sides of that fence and I do not want to be the 'other man'." Jean-Claude replied. Ge looked down at Jean-Claude and said, "We can still be friends though can't we? I would really like that." Jean-Claude smiled and said, "Yes, just give me a few days to process what just happened and it will be okay." Ge smiled and said, "Good. I will be going to China in a few days and will be back in four months."

Jean-Claude and Ge traded emails while he was gone to China. One day the Jean-Claude's cell phone rang and he looked and Ge's name popped up. Jean-Claude pushed the ignore button because he was surprised to get a call – Ge must be back. Sure enough, when Jean-Claude listened to the message, Ge was back in California. Jean-Claude never called Ge back, he didn't feel comfortable seeing Ge when he knew there was a boyfriend back in China that did not know what Ge was doing here in

California. Jean-Claude kept thinking about how he had felt about infidelity and the hurt that it causes; he could knowingly not be a part of it.

"That Ge was one hot man Jean-Claude, but I'm glad you stood your ground and didn't get yourself into another one of those triangle things." Ms. Wauneta pointedly stated.

For whatever reason, this phone call was the trigger. Jean-Claude began a faster descent into the dark recesses of depression. He held it at bay for several months and kept stuffing his emotions down every time they would try to surface. Finally, one day while working on his computer and listening to music a song started playing on his iPod. Jean-Claude had heard this song a dozen times before, but for some reason he stopped and really listened to the words of the song. The song was The Touch by Ricky Martin and he started to think of Sam; no one else just Sam.

The process had begun – depression fully took hold and the feelings could no longer be kept in the box, it began overflowing with the years and years of crammed feelings that he had not dealt over of his lifetime. One by one they crept out like monsters in the dark seeking a victim any victim. However, the only one they could find to torment was Jean-Claude. These were, after all, his own monsters he had been running away from all these years.

Jean-Claude became extremely despondent, refused to speak to anyone, would barely look at passing strangers, nothing could make him smile, he felt hopeless as his mind continued to grapple with all these thoughts and emotions flowing over him. Jean-Claude was having a difficult time eating because every time he went to eat the tears would start and he would feel sick to his stomach.

With encouragement from a couple of Veterans Jean-Claude had befriended, and following their suggestion. Jean-

Claude finally asked for help from a professional and began the process of attempting to work through all the issues he had stuffed inside for so many years. Jean-Claude was about to embark on the long process of self-discovery and healing.

Reflections

Jean-Claude began examining his life but it kept coming to him out of order and in a convoluted manner. He was having a difficult time keeping things in perspective and it was chaos. Finally he sat down and began writing a list to get some organization to his thoughts.

In looking back Jean-Claude smiled when he thought of all the people that had come into his life over the years. "I've had a unique and eclectic group of individuals visit my life and I've really learned so much from them over the years." Jean-Claude thought.

To start there was his family: a biological mother that checked out and went on her own leaving a small child with his father. Jean-Claude considered himself lucky to have grown up with his father; it was unheard of in those days for a mother to lose custody of the children. Sure, his stepmother was not the perfect parent, but she did the best she knew how and Jean-Claude readily admitted that he was not the easiest child to rear. He had made her life a living hell every chance he got, out of spite. He dearly missed having a relationship with his little brother and sister, but because of his stepmother's decision, he stayed out of their lives. Even though Jean-Claude misses the family connection, he is comfortable on his own away from the family dynamics.

In the military he found a great friend in Brad and misses him all the time because he was like a brother to Jean-Claude. However, Jean-Claude will always cherish his memories of Brad. If Jean-Claude was to be honest with himself he would have realized that he developed, at the least, a massive crush and, at most, was in love with Brad.

While in the military he met and fell in love for the first time in his life with Sam. While he handled the relationship

170

horribly, Jean-Claude began to realize just how much that brief relationship with Sam had affected his entire life in ways he could never had imagined. Jean-Claude was so ill-equipped to deal with the raw pure love that Sam offered that he ended up destroying everything. How Jean-Claude continued looking for men that shared the same qualities he had found so attractive in Sam and caused him to fall in love with him. Jean-Claude discovered that choices do have consequences, and sometimes those choices severely affect the people we love.

All the drag queens in Jean-Claude's life have always given him hope that one day he can be as free and confident as they are every day. Jean-Claude found it interesting how all along the journey there has always been at least one drag queen in his life. His first exposure with this confidence was with Sam and the theme continues; Jean-Claude is jealous of all of them because of this self-confidence.

Jean-Claude even found through all his relationships with men he could grow as a person and each boyfriend brought something different to his life. With each of them he continued growing, sometimes not in a good way or on a forward path; sometimes it went sideways in a drastic fashion. He discovered what his limits were in a relationship, how much he was willing to sacrifice to be with someone and the things that were just beyond his limits.

When Jean-Claude was younger he could easily go into a rage if he finally hit his limits; however, this rage was on the inside and would begin plotting his revenge. The focus of his ire would not necessarily know it was him that was causing their discomfort and problems. If he was angry enough he would push back directly on the person and, in his mind, it was thermal nuclear warfare with a scorched earth policy – nothing would survive. This process can last months, but unfazed by the time involved Jean-Claude he would not be dissuaded from his goal. This was a cause for him to terminate several relationships when some could have been repaired over time and with honest and sincere discussions. Jean-Claude has mellowed out significantly has he has aged.

Jean-Claude continues to struggle with being completely out in both his private and professional life. He does care what people think of him and is afraid to show who he really is in life. When he hears a conversation or even when he is in the conversation where something anti-gay is mentioned he feels uncomfortable. However, Jean-Claude often chuckles and thinks to himself, "It is funny they are saying this stuff in front of me – they have no clue I'm gay. I wonder if they knew would they say something different." Jean-Claude had always had the ability to move between both the gay and straight worlds of his life. He always made certain that they never collided; there were never any friends in both worlds. He had worked at a couple of companies that had other gay employees, but those work acquaintances would never cross over into his private life, ever.

When Jean-Claude finally started a Facebook account and was filling out the profile information there was a check box entitled, "Likes (a) men or (b) women." Jean-Claude looked at the question for a little while and left it blank. He was hiding his true self again. Several days later he went back and checked the box "likes men." Jean-Claude thought, "What the hell, got to take a step in the right direction sometime. Besides, I have accepted friend requests from several drag queens and people can connect them anyway."

Jean-Claude had often used one-night stands, hookups and the famous "Catch and Release Program" to feel loved or cared about. By using sex to replace love, Jean-Claude was setting himself up for failure because he was not addressing the core issues; Jean-Claude didn't feel he was entitled to love someone completely. The ambiguous sexual encounters allowed him to feel euphoric for the moment. But like any drug, once it was gone, he would begin the search all again to get that euphoric feeling back.

Jean-Claude has found it interesting how much his relationship with Sam, however short and tumultuous, has affected all the relationships in his life. From the first physical attraction or a personality trait Jean-Claude might see all tied back to Sam. Jean-Claude discovered while reflecting if a person didn't have a quality he had admired in Sam, he would not get involved with the guy.

Although through this entire process, Jean-Claude discovered that he was still in love with Sam. To what extent Jean-Claude didn't know but to discover 20 years later he still had feelings for Sam was a surprise to Jean-Claude. Was it the idea of being with Sam in general? Was it the security he felt when he was with Sam? Was it simply because Sam was Jean-Claude's "first?" The more Jean-Claude thought about this the more he became confused.

> Ms. Wauneta patted Jean-Claude's hand and asked, "So do you know where Sam lives?" Jean-Claude looked and replied, "No." As Ms. Wauneta stood up and walked out of the room, she called back "Well let's look up Sam on the computer. Are you coming Chickie?" Jean-Claude followed knowing it would be useless to argue once she got an idea in her head. As Jean-Claude entered the office, Ms. Wauneta exclaimed, "Hey, there he is! Oh my, cute too." Jean-Claude rushed over to the computer to take a look. Ms. Wauneta said, "Sit and write an email right now." Jean-Claude looked at her in amazement. "I mean it, write!" Ms. Wauneta said while poking Jean-Claude in the arm. Jean-Claude typed a short message and sat looking at the screen. Ms. Wauneta leaned over and jabbed the

'enter' key with her long red nail while saying, "There, now you can sit and wait for a response. It is done Chickie." There was nothing Jean-Claude could do now, the email had been sent.

Ms. Wauneta asked Jean-Claude: "If Sam asked you to move to where he lived, without any guarantee that things would work out, or even if there would be a relationship; would you?" Jean-Claude answered, "It depends…" "No, would you?" she demanded. Jean-Claude responded, "If he said he liked me and if there was even a small chance of a relationship with Sam, sure, but he wouldn't ask that, not after all this time anyway." Ms. Wauneta rolled her eyes, sighing heavily she said, "There you go again, thinking too much and analyzing everything. You are so afraid to take a risk; that you might get hurt. We all get hurt at some point and you are going to have to take a chance somewhere along the line again you know. Just stop thinking and let your heart take you where it is going to take you and stop fighting. Don't you think you have been fighting long enough? I swear to God if the opportunity ever presents itself and you wuss out, I'm kicking you in the ass." Jean-Claude laughed for the first time in a long time as the image of this tiny drag queen kicking him in the ass while on four inch heels. The sad part of that image was the fact Ms. Wauneta could probably kick his ass with very little effort.

www.ingramcontent.com/pod-product-compliance
Lightning Source LLC
Chambersburg PA
CBHW072145270326
41931CB00010B/1893